JFK to 9/11

EVERYTHING IS A

Rich Man's Trick

Francis Richard Conolly

JFK to 911 Everything Is A Rich Man's Trick
Copyright ©2018, 2021 Francis Richard Conolly

Published by:
Trine Day LLC
PO Box 577
Walterville, OR 97489
1-800-556-2012
www.TrineDay.com
trineday@icloud.com

Library of Congress Control Number: 2021943949

Conolly, Richard.
JFK to 911 Everything Is A Rich Man's Trick – 1st ed.
p. cm.
Epub (ISBN-13) 978-1-63424-375-9
Print (ISBN-13) 978-1-63424-374-2
1.Kennedy, John F. -- (John Fitzgerald), -- 1917-1963 -- Assassination. 2. September 11 Terrorist Attacks, 2001. 3. Conspiracies -- United States. 4. HISTORY / United States / 20th Century. 5. Order of Skull & Bones. 6. Political Science -- Political Freedom & Security -- Terrorism. 7. War criminals -- United States. 8. Fascism -- United States. 9. Social Science/ Conspiracy Theories. I. Title

First Edition
10 9 8 7 6 5 4 3 2 1

Printed in South Korea
Distribution to the Trade by:
Independent Publishers Group (IPG)
814 North Franklin Street
Chicago, Illinois 60610
312.337.0747
www.ipgbook.com

PUBLISHER'S FOREWORD

Where, oh where has my little dog gone?
Oh where, oh where can he be?
With his ears cut short
And his tail cut long
Oh where, oh where can he be?

Perhaps the man over there will know
He may have seen him go by
Who knows where he might have decided to go
But we've got to give it a try

The Kennedy Assassination has been bedeviling the world ever since it occured that sunny day in Dallas in November 1963. *A day that changed everything.*

I was in school that day. The announcement came over the public-address system, and the shock started to set in. It was Spanish class, and the class had a TV set, which was soon turned on – our national nightmare began. Then within five minutes came a sputtering PA request for me to go to the principal's office. What had *I* done? I get there, and find my "paper boss." He took me out of school and put me on the street selling newspapers. I had been delivering papers on my bicycle daily for several years and continued for several more afterwards, but only on this day, and then two day later, when Oswald was shot and killed live on national TV – was I on the street hawking news. The assassination was/is traumatic. We are still living with the horror, and its cascading effects upon our nation's journey and psyche. We lost more than our innocence…

Time moved on: Vietnam, Watergate, Iran hostage crisis, October Surprise, an assassination attempt on Reagan, Iran/Contra, Monica Lewinsky, hanging chads – and then another day *that changed everything…*

September 11, 2001 – 9/11 has engendered a whole new generation of "conspiracy theorists," seeking to understand and explain the event: How does our world really work?

Francis Richard Conolly produced a nearly three-and-a-half-hour film in 2018, *Everything Is a Rich Man's Trick,* which soon went viral racking up huge numbers on YouTube. As the world turned, and the political divides heated up, calls were made to censor disinformation and conspiracy theories on the Interent. Soon, *Everything Is a Rich Man's Trick* became harder to view online, and people's frustrations grew.

We live in a world with many competing beliefs. There are folks, who for religious reasons, claim that the world is only between 6,000 and 10,000 years old. There is a book, *Mortal Error: The Shot that Killed JFK,* published by a major US publisher in 1993 that posits the theory that JFK's fatal shot was fired accidently by a US Secret Service agent. The book is a complete myth, but it hasn't been censored or "deplatformed." In the US, our constuitution gives us the right to free speech, but doesn't guarantee us that everything said or printed is correct. It is up to us to examine and use discernment.

Having studied the JFK assassination and other US scandals for many years, I find Mr. Conolly's basic premise sound, but I believe he has erred in some of his details of the deed. All researchers make mistakes along the way, myself included. But that doesn't mean one shouldn't read or watch, for without experience – how does one know anything? This is an important work to help us understand our history.

The adage "the devil is in the details" derives from an earlier German proverb – *"Der liebe Gott steckt im detail,"* which translates as "God is in the detail." How does a devil change places with "God"?

> *O dear, what can the matter be?*
> *O dear, what can the matter be?*
> *O dear, what can the matter be?*
> *Johnny's so long at the fair.*

Onwards to the Utmost of Futures
Peace,
R.A. "Kris" Millegan
Publisher
TrineDay
July 29, 2021

Murder most foul, as in the best it is. But this most foul, strange and unnatural.
– Ghost, *Hamlet*, William Shakespeare

TABLE OF CONTENTS

Prologue 1

Foreword 5

The Book: JFK to 911 Everything Is A Rich Man's Trick 19

Afterword 111

Bibliography 133

Index...135

About the Author...139

PROLOGUE

Movie buffs are well aware that many great feature films were a great book first. The greatest international hits of all time, like *The Godfather, The Beguiled, Cool Hand Luke* and *One Flew Over The Cuckoo's Nest* were all highly revered works of literature before they were turned into films, so it is most unusual to see, within these pages, the process happening in reverse.

For those who are unaware, and I think by now that few will be, *JFK to 911 Everything Is A Rich Man's Trick* became an internationally-acclaimed cult feature film in spite of YouTube's efforts to disguise it's popularity by under-reporting the hits by over two hundred times.

However, the main purpose of this prologue is to make the reader aware that books have their limitations. It's very hard for a book to convey action, because it is not a moving image. These pages obviously cannot put across everything that the film contains; so I can only hope that all who read it will feel outraged that the establishment has done so much to keep the movie out of public view (Both President Donald Trump and the Queen of England acted to ban it.) and to use that outrage positively to do all they can in the future to make sure that anyone who wants to see the film can have the chance to see it.

What you are about to read is, essentially, the shooting script of *JFK to 911: Everything Is A Rich Man's Trick,"* a feature documentary which for some considerable time now has been shaking the political world to a degree that few artistic works have ever achieved. Whilst no-one knows the exact figure (save for Susan Wojcicki) it seems likely that it has been watched well over a billion times, and the true figure may well be considerably greater.

It is now in print due to nothing other than rabid public demand.

Many people, on every continent, seem to feel the words by themselves are of cardinal importance.

I would invite anyone considering reading this book to examine the public comments sections beneath the multitude of pirate copies of my movie which can still be found online. They all echo the consistent refrain that this is a work of art which desperately needs to be shared by absolutely everyone on planet Earth. As one would expect the inhabitants of the USA have said over and over again that it ought to be made available "in every American school and on every American college campus."

They feel this way because so many Americans have agreed it is a "moment of epiphany" in the history of their country. A moment when a sleep-walking people woke up to what their country really is; and to what their leaders have been doing to them since that terrible day in Dallas when a nation lost the best man it ever knew.

I want to use this opportunity to thank all those who have tried their utmost to give me support, respect and encouragement since the movie went viral. In particular I want to extend much feeling to those strong and enterprising souls who invited me on to their Internet chat-shows to try to make sure the truth movement maintained it's momentum. The conversations I have had with Broadcasters like Justin Stellman, Patrick Timpone, Jason Goodman, Charlie Robinson, Ricky Varandas, Addy Adakin and the TruthZilla team have all turned out to be of critical importance as the Trump administration unravelled and the Epstein/Maxwell/Prince Andrew scandal became the daily fixation of mainstream news globally.

I want to extend the same feeling to the hordes of people who, like the amazing mother-of-six Claire Calvey (she's Irish) have used social media both to lend moral support and also try to spread my message. I am now in a position of having to ask them all to do just one thing more: which is to somehow try to reach out to absolutely every good soul who has seen my movie and ask them to please pay now for what I originally gave them for free on YouTube by buying a copy of this book. It is my estimate that a bare minimum of some 250 million people must have seen the movie, some of them more than a dozen times. If absolutely everyone who has watched the film version of this work purchases a copy of the book it will become financially viable to take foreign-language translations into European and Asian Cinemas. Non-English speakers throughout the world will finally get the chance to enjoy *JFK to 911* and, through this means, accumulate revenues which will allow me to produce the Part 2, which everyone wants to see. Those who have demonstrated such unbounded enthusiasm for my work will, I am sure, agree that the German people in particular must now be given the chance to finally learn the true history of their own country by discovering the true mechanism through which Hitler ascended to power.

The dirty rich people do everything they can on a daily basis to discredit the idea that upon this earth we all are (or could be) just one great family of man. As George Orwell astutely observed, nothing frightens them more than the idea of a world full of free and equal human beings living together in harmony.

To this end they have done everything in their power to also discredit my work, and prevent it from reaching the public. But just as decent Americans, and Australians, and Canadians have done their level best to share my thoughts and words with their Brothers and Sisters in their own homelands, it is now the responsibility of English speakers everywhere to share what follows with their Brothers and Sisters in Germany, France, Spain and Italy, and to push out from there into the whole of Europe, Asia and Africa.

Because those who have said the entire world needs this book are not wrong. Every working man on earth today is toiling and suffering under the same secret Fascist cabal. It is time for the entire world to find out who these secret Fascists are, and how they operate.

FOREWORD

Anyone who is coming to this story for the very first time may well benefit from knowing a little about the history of how this Book came into the world. The Rock Star known as Sting reminisced in one of his songs how his "mother cried when President Kennedy died" and it was exactly the same for me, which in itself is a little ironic because Sting and I both harken from the same town (Wallsend).

Imagine if you will a six year-old little boy standing before one of those wood-encased black and white Televisions, utterly bewildered as to why the normally stoic British TV presenters were sobbing and shaking with shock, while his mother and grim-visaged father sat on the settee behind him crying their eyes out. Try to imagine an entire community so traumatised you would have thought every child in the district had been simultaneously run over and killed. Try to imagine how it would feel to attend the mass funeral of all those thousands of little innocents, and you might just begin to grasp the outpouring of grief at the death of John Fitzgerald Kennedy.

It lasted for months. Every adult I knew shared my father's grim visage. And as they stared over and over again at what I later came to know was the Orville Nix Film on those black-and-white TV screens, a consensus grew. The adults towering over me were in agreement. "They've killed him because he would have given the poor people a chance."

They? I thought. Who were "They"? I asked politely for explanations. The adults lit their cigarettes, sipped their Whisky, blew out slow smoke-rings and told me that children should be seen and not heard. At that moment I knew, somehow, that I was never going to be the same again. Something which should have lived had been stillborn, and I *had* to find out who was responsible.

My own personal universe at that time was tiny: as tiny as I was. All I knew was a back garden where we grew rhubarb to save money. Two doors down the neighbours had chickens. One of the chickens had an eye torn out by a cat. In a street bordered by big green hedges ours was the only Council House which had yellow privet. It gave me the feeling that somehow my family was different.

Over time I broke that lovely yellow hedge by kicking a football into it for hours on end, much to my Father's annoyance, and I always felt that it was a punishment for my various misdemeanours that on gloomy Sunday mornings we were hauled, smartly dressed, down to a decrepit old Chapel where I sat bored for hours and contemplated the "Stations of the Cross."

This was a series of paintings which went right around the walls, and in this 21st Century of ours an educational Psychologist would insist they were highly unsuitable images for children. Ostensibly an attempt to retail the march to Calvary and the Crucifixion, every single picture gloated in the most frightening way over whipping, flogging, torture, multiple penetration with the 'crown of thorns' scourging, beating, lashing, flagellating, and finally the great joyful climax of death itself.

Up until December of 1963 I had simply accepted this as our life. But the Kennedy assassination made me see it all differently. This was many years before I even heard the word "sadomasochism," but I suddenly knew what all of it really represented. My gaze was transfixed on those hideous pictures of dripping blood while my callow, childish mind was still thinking about JFK's blood spilling out on to the streets of Dallas. So this is what grown-ups are really into, I thought. This is the real world. It was the very first time that I had become conscious of the whole world as one place: and by the manner of his death John F. Kennedy had given me a lesson in what kind of world it was.

The feeling never went away. And it was reinforced five years later when first Martin Luther King and then Bobby met the same fate. I was barely eleven, and I was watching my mother's heart breaking for a second and then a third time. Then came my next big moment of epiphany. In the early sixties everyone got married. Even the Beatles. It felt like barely a month would pass before yet another fleet of ribbon-garlanded Rolls-Royce's would glide regally into our street, and it was traditional for the bride and groom in those days to throw a big pile of copper pennies and thrupenny bits out of the windows of the wedding car as it drove away, so that the children could fight one another on the ground for pocket-money and buy sweets with it. As the fastest runner I usually did better out of it than anyone, even once buying a bicycle with the proceeds of one particularly lucrative scramble.

But after JFK, and then MLK, and then his brother, something was different. It felt like we were living under a massive black cloud which would never go away, and as yet another wedding car moved off and the usual hailstorm of coins sent a gaggle of screaming children diving on to the brick-hard cement I hesitated. "Go on Francis!" the adults yelled "that's chocolate money!" But I couldn't move.

A few days earlier on BBC Television I had seen the Dictator of Haiti, Papa Doc Duvalier, riding through Port-au-Prince in an identical Rolls-Royce. He too was throwing money out of his car window, except that the pack chasing him were not children but grown women. Dressed in rags and obviously suffering in atrocious poverty the women ran after the car for mile after mile while the grinning Dictator sprayed his largesse – and for the first time in my life I understood why. Duvalier was telling the BBC reporter this was a "demonstration of his love for his people" but, as he laughed just like a hyena at the panting, sweat-soaked, totally exhausted mothers clawing at each other for money they desperately needed to feed their starving children, I knew what this was really all about. The intention was to *humiliate* those women. Just as the wedding cars were there to humiliate us. My traumatic childhood, punctuated as it was by political assassinations, had made me into a thinking man before I was twelve. I was left wondering; who was paying Papa Doc to humiliate those women? Whose idea was it? And who would want to humiliate me? And why?

I realised I had developed a habit of taking thought, wherein instead of simply *engaging* in everything like the other children I became aware that I was *evaluating* everything, and it was with this attitude that I found myself judging the first history book I had to study about the Kennedy assassination when I was carted off to prison for being a naughty boy (actually it was a Boarding School, but it was hardly different to prison)

It was tripe. Although I was barely adolescent the writing seemed clumsy and wordy to me, and the moment it got around to mentioning the "Communist Fanatic Oswald" there was a distinct odour of falsehood. One got the impression that the wordy text was saying Lee Harvey Oswald *definitely* fired the shots, and that no-one in their right mind could ever doubt this was anything other than historical fact. Oh dear, I thought. Why be so insistent? I remembered the trouble my Father had taken over teaching me Shakespeare's immortal line "methinks he doth protest too much" and in English class we had just finished Orwell's *Animal Farm* and had made a start on *1984,* so I asked my teachers whether this utter cowpat of a History Book could have been something devised by Winston Smith as he toiled in the Ministry of Truth? For how did they *know* for certain that it was not compiled with exactly the same intent to deceive? But my Teachers had no idea what I was talking about. So I read to them, out loud, that critical passage from Chapter 4 of Orwell's dystopian novel where Winston Smith begins to realise that in many ways his girlfriend, Julia, is more astute than he is when she tells him she is certain that the missiles (or rocket-bombs as Orwell called them in *1984*) which constantly bombard London are not fired by the enemy Super-State East Asia at all, but by the rulers of their own Super-State Oceania "just so as to keep the population living in constant fear."

In the text Winston Smith reflects that this was something "which had literally never occurred to him," and now I perceived that my teachers had exactly the same mentality. They simply did not possess the wit to imagine that the world could possibly be different to what they had been told the world was. They had been brought up to believe that the British never tell lies because that was what the Nazis did, so they just swallowed it whole, and never, ever, thought about it.

This was only weeks after another history class where we had studied one of those dreadful "Ladybird" books entitled *Life In Hitler's Germany*. I can vividly recall the illustrations depicting the well-groomed wholesome, civilized German families eating their Sunday Roast together – and opposite more pictures of the same people kitted-out in Swastika-festooned Black Nazi Livery. "Gentle Husbands, Fathers and their sons put on uniforms and became vicious killers" the caption ran. We had to read it together. Then the teachers asked us to explain how this could have happened? How could this screaming little defective Hitler, with his silly little toothbrush-moustache, have single-handedly convinced not one but several great nations to inflict such bestial atrocities upon the world? We were all bemused. "Aren't you supposed to tell us?" we retorted. But then it became abundantly clear to me that the teachers were asking because, just as with the JFK conspiracy, they had absolutely no idea.

It seemed to me that they were genuinely hoping that one of us might really turn out to be the boy who saw the King's new clothes so they could finally find out for themselves why six-million lives were extinguished in the gas chambers. But they were simply clueless. Useless. And the thought occurred to me. Might that be the whole idea?

Fast-forward to 1988 and the 25th anniversary of the Kennedy assassination. In the intervening years I had consumed every scrap of information I could find from books, periodicals and magazine articles. They all gave me the impression that they were trying to hide much more than they were trying to reveal, hence it came as no surprise when Time/Life investigator Josiah Thompson concluded the *Men Who Killed Kennedy* documentary by explaining that this had been a murder case quite unlike any other in human history. From his decades of private investigator work he had deduced that all murder cases conform to a similar pattern. Any experienced detective will tell you that over a period of time every homicide becomes less and less complex. It may take years, but gradually, one by one, suspects are eliminated, conflicting scenarios evaporate, and the range of possibilities narrows. Things get more simple. Always. And yet, as Josiah Thompson ruefully reflected, not only had the JFK assassination not become more simple over time, there appeared instead to be increasing complexity. Only one rational explanation was possible. Someone out there, some dark force, was deliberately manufacturing that increasing complexity. So who were they? and what could they possibly have to lose after twenty five years?

My breakthrough as a professional writer with the BBC had not, unfortunately, provided me with sufficient funds that I might attempt to answer this burning question. And it was also becoming clear from the way in which I was being treated (the BBC did their utmost to try and force me to write those dreadful soapy medical dramas) that the professional mainstream media were keen to steer me away from anything that might involve truth-seeking. But then came the dawn of the Internet Age.

I remember pulling my first computer out of it's styrofoam box and plugging in my very first broadband cable. As a life-long movie buff I found myself thinking at that very moment about a poignant scene from the *Birdman of Alcatraz* in which Robert F. Stroud unpacked his very first Laboratory microscope in his jail cell. The Film's narrator said it became "the light he had been waiting for" and I wondered if this slim little laptop might be about to play a similar role in my own life?

Within days my movie-buff curiousity had rekindled my appetite for true-crime. I found myself revisiting the 1976 feature film *All The President's Men* and researching all the characters I would have liked to have known much more about way back then: for who was G. Gordon Liddy? And E. Howard Hunt? Who was Muskie? and Magruder? and Bob Haldeman? They weren't even seen in the film itself, and yet every one was a central character in one of the most disgraceful episodes in American political history. So I googled them all, and swiftly found myself staring, like one of those cartoon characters who has just walked off a cliff and is suspended in mid-air, at a YouTube video in which E. Howard Hunt was making a death-bed confession about his involvement in the Kennedy assassination plot.

My blood filled with ice. But it swiftly melted. What if, I thought, this is just more disinformation? Just another cynical attempt by the same old dirty people to use a dying man, and the weight generally given to death-bed confessions in law-courts, for their own purposes? For who could even say that this truly was the voice of the real Howard Hunt? What if he had already died and this was an actor playing a role?

Several emails to Bob Woodward of the *Washington Post*, enquiring as to why the media were not going ape-shit over this confession video yielded no response. And as I watched the loop of BBC Film which was showing over and over and over what appeared to be a commercial airliner flying in to the World Trade Centre I knew I suddenly had a huge amount of work to do.

The Internet connected me to journalists, historians and researchers whose names I had never heard before, like John Hankey, John Buchanan, Webster Tarpley, Jeff Rense, John Loftus, Anton Chaitkin,

John Simkin, Professor Antony Sutton, and a sweet little English Historian called John Costello. It was primarily Costello's Books which had led to the excellent Channel 4 Documentary *Edward VIII: The Traitor King* and having finally found the missing piece to the entire Kennedy assassination mystery in the work of the sagacious and tenderhearted Robert D. Morningstar, and completed the first draft of my screenplay, I felt my best chance of getting the film made was to get in touch with John Costello and try through him to approach Channel 4, as we had clearly been working on different segments of the same puzzle. So I googled his name.

My blood filled with ice for a second time.

John Costello was dead. He had been assassinated by someone who sprayed a bio-toxin on his food while he ate a restaurant meal.

As he was English, and had proved beyond all doubt that Edward VIII was a Fascist and Nazi collaborator, I felt it was far more likely that MI5 were responsible for his demise than the Central Intelligence Agency. I have never been naive', but up to that point in my own life I had never thought the Queen of England would have a man assassinated just for writing a book because, lets face it, hardly anyone reads. But there it was. Costello had quite likely been trying to bring out what I had now brought out in my film script and had died for it. I was therefore scarcely surprised when I set out to try and get the Film commissioned and found no-one would touch it with a barge-pole.

And it was not just the major networks like the BBC and ITV who sniffed and turned away. The long reach of the "Tentacles of the Fascist Octopus" even stretched into the institutions who were deliberately set-up to help talented British film producers who were short of funds. The head of the British Flim Institute at that time, Amanda Nevill, refused to take my calls. I was able to actually visit the Screen Yorkshire offices in Leeds, but all they did was shake their heads, and when the chief of Creative England told me he was going to do his utmost to get my movie produced he was promptly fired. For many months it felt like I had no-one to turn to.

But then I got a big surprise. I had videotaped a documentary called *O.J. The Untold Story* which had very skilfully revealed to the world the true killer of Nicole Brown Simpson and Ron Goldman, and took a chance on writing to the producer, Malcom Brinkworth, simply because his Film seemed to hold the pursuit of truth as being above all other things. To my utter astonishment something I said struck a chord with him, and in the following months we had many meetings, at British Academy of Film and Television Arts (BAFTA) in London, at his office in Richmond, and his home base in Bath. At first all seemed well. Malcom told me the budget would be around two-million pounds, we were going to make "the definitive Kennedy assassination movie" together, and he was confident of getting the money from "a girl he was on very good terms with at Channel 4."

However, at our last meeting I mentioned that my ongoing research indicated that all those involved in the Kennedy plot, and all those entrusted with keeping the truth covered-up ever since, are all pedophiles. Instant big freeze-out. I had said something wrong. Malcom suddenly became boorish, and, wildly gesticulating in a manner which really caught me off-guard, insisted that "if we're going down that route I shall be out of the door in one half-second!" I would love to be able to say right here that I never saw or heard from Malcom ever again. What was so very terrible was that every time we spoke on the phone after that it became more and more obvious that he had been ordered to string me along, so that I would hopefully become disillusioned and give up. That particular phase ended when I met up with the wonderful, honest man with whom I finally managed to make the film. And it goes without saying that instead of a two million budget we had no money whatsoever.

It would be tempting at this point to provide a blow-by-blow account of the way in which every single film distribution company, both foreign and domestic, refused to give *JFK to 911* a chance in public cinemas. I must have written tens of thousands of emails to the Germans, Swedes, French and the Dutch, but I think by now that anyone reading this will have grasped the essential point, which is that our mainstream media is corrupt to the marrow of it's bones. We therefore had no other choice but to put the movie out on YouTube where, I think it is safe to say, it almost melted the Internet.

In what felt like no time at all the hits reached a million: then two million. Every man and his dog seemed to be either reviewing it or ripping it off. The heavy-metal rock band Travis Warren and the Texas Lights brought out a pop song entitled "Everything Is A Rich Man's Trick" and compliments and salutations claiming this was nothing less than the "greatest and most important Documentary ever made" came pouring in from places as far and wide as Portugal, Canada, Australia, India and even China; whereupon the hosts of the many Internet chat-shows inevitably sat-up and took notice. I was interviewed first by Richie Allen, and still firmly believe that the "murder" of British M.P. Jo Cox, which was reported just minutes before we went on air, was a staged event to get people looking the wrong way on that particular night. The Establishment very obviously did not want interest either in me or the Film to grow any further – going so far as to ban my next two interviews: on the Australian *Rodrigo Soto Show* and on *Raconteurs News*. But worse was yet to come.

I learned whilst broadcasting live-on-air that YouTube had been deliberately under-reporting the hits by over two hundred times, the true figure being way over a billion, and then? The big news came. The movie was banned altogether. YouTube had blacked it out on the ludicrous pretext that too many people had been using the public comments section in an effort to spread anti-Semitic propaganda (Susan Wojcicki having clearly never imagined that the CIA were writing the Jew-baiting comments themselves). But the Anglo-American establishment had made a huge mistake. They had not realised just how many shrewd observers had seen the ban coming, and in the months that followed wonderful souls like Shane Seavey and Alexander Avella simply uploaded pirate copies from their hard-drives. It sent the Establishment into a tailspin.

They now knew my work had acted like a flash-flood. A raging torrent had swept through the silted-up sewer that is Western Politics and made the waters of Democracy crystal clear for the first time in modern history. The entire population could suddenly see exactly what the Oligarchs really are! And what they are really up to! The spies who listen to ordinary people's conversations in pubs and parks and shopping malls were reporting back to their intelligence agency bosses that the schism which had previously existed in society; the divide which had split down the middle all those who believed in government conspiracy and all those who did not, was over. The bus drivers and nurses and bricklayers were suddenly all in agreement that the mainstream media could no longer be trusted because they were all simply retailing "fake news." The beleaguered heads of the Anglo-American Establishment simply *had* to do something. And bloody quick.

It was this set of circumstances which led directly to that very strange evening which everyone, I have found, seems to remember so very vividly; when Donald Trump suddenly started yelling "You're Fake News! You're Fake News!" over and over again at the TV Cameras. Many commentators at the time seriously wondered if he was beginning to lose his marbles, because they couldn't fathom why he was so very suddenly going off the deep end? What that incident was essentially all about was that the Central Intelligence Agency had sat Trump down and said "You have to listen very carefully Mr. President ... this goddamned Conolly dude is shafting us. His movie has woken everybody up to our dirty little game and made them see that all the news we put out is fake. The only way we can think of to effectively retaliate is to make the counter-claim that all *Alternative* media is fake i.e. that it is all just click-bait. So get out there and face the press and do your level best to muddy the waters again, because that's your only real purpose. You understand?" It must have seemed at the time that it was the only thing they could do – and it backfired spectacularly.

Because when the American people saw Trump's little hissy-fit it became clear that their universal reaction was "Oh no no no no no! Mr. President. *You* are the one who is fake" In other words it succeeded only in giving Trump a Richard Nixon moment.

Foreword

No American will ever forget that seminal evening at the height of Watergate when Trick Dicky Nixon went on national TV in a last-ditch attempt to clear his name. "Many people are claiming I'm a Crook!" he bellowed "Well I'm not a Crook!" The American people shook their heads as one man and said "No Mr. Nixon, you *are* a filthy Crook" and in doing his level best to muddy the waters again Trump had succeeded only in tarring himself with the same brush. It is for this reason that the mainstream media has recently become even more ridiculous; and even more replete with stupid stories, witless issues, and utterly pointless debates. We were all used to hearing ridiculous garbage about giant rats living in the sewers, and anecdotes about women making thousands of pounds every day by working as nude domestic cleaners in the rich boroughs of London and Paris. But the "awakening" caused by my film; a national moment of epiphany wherein entire populations have taken off their rose-tinted spectacles and accepted they are living under Fascist, Totalitarian rule has led to a corresponding increase in the levels of lunacy we had become accustomed to on mainstream media. For does anyone think it was just a co-incidence that the Establishment chose this moment to wheel out Caitlin Jenner? and demand that the general public start debating utter tripe like whether there ought to be separate toilets for transgender people?

They felt they had to do this because they had already worn out gay rights, black rights, women's rights and immigrants rights as distraction stories; so there was nothing else left for the propaganda mills to grind up. And it has been highly noticeable how the Oligarchs have even tried to change the meanings of words in modern parlance in order to maintain themselves in power. When the public comments section of the original version of my film first began to fill-up with claims that "this movie should be shown in every history class as part of the American curriculum" it was generally agreed that a new "woke" culture had grown up of people who were now wide-awake, to the same degree that even George Orwell would be if he were around now, to the reality that every single aspect of Western civilized life – the Justice system; the educational system; the economic system and most importantly the mass media, is just one gigantic hoax: and our Democracy nothing more than a carefully crafted illusion – a web spun by those in authority to dupe all of us every single minute of every single day for ever and ever.

Of course to an elitist, Fascist Establishment such crystal-clear understanding as this was simply intolerable. Hence they have been doing their utmost to contaminate language itself by trying to convince the public that someone who is 'woke' is not at all an educated, sceptical, discriminating individual who now sees Western political life for the ongoing fraud that it is, but is actually the kind of illiterate nutcase who wants to argue interminably about pointless trivia like homosexual and transgender and immigrant rights. That is why breakfast TV presenters in particular have spent so much time on this nonsense; and also why so many people have noticed that every discussion programme these days has an allegedly homosexual coloured person in their team. The function of the limp-wristed man endlessly talking camp is to act as a constant reminder that we the audience are meant to accept without question the notion that the whole world is now supposedly a place wherein we must never do or say or think anything which someone from a "minority" might find "offensive." This is how they now try to control our every thought, and it is the daily business of modern media to try always to lob this completely *perverted* notion of what a "wokist" is into a melting pot with words like "Liberal," "Socialist," "Conservative," "Left-Wing" etc. Today all of these words are deliberately being used disingenuously.

There was once a time when pretty much anyone could have gone on TV and defined "Conservative" as basically meaning Right-Wing: it's adherents being those who believed in absolute rights to private property, their rights to make as much private profit as they desired without state interference, and low, if any, taxation for those who showed the most "enterprise." Bound up with these notions went less clearly-stated ideals that all welfare should be suspended, as hard-working wealth-creating citizens should not be asked to "carry" those who are lazy and therefore a drag upon society. Left-wingers, by contrast, are meant to believe in state welfare, and state support for those who, through no fault of their own, have found themselves unemployed, disenfranchised or suffering ill-health. It follows naturally that a Conservative understands the word "freedom" only in the context of freedom to exploit others for profit, while the Left-winger understands freedom as meaning freedom from exploitation. A liberal, when I was at school, simply meant someone who thought it was a good idea for everyone to enjoy as much freedom of all kinds as was practically possible.

But today such clarity as this is being consciously undermined. Statements and beliefs which would never have been ascribed to anyone Left-Wing even ten years ago are bandied about constantly. The BBC is endlessly described as "Lefty" and "woke" by disinformation agents in spurious YouTube videos precisely because those entrusted with running the propaganda campaign know the BBC could not be more Right-Wing than it is at present; especially in the way it protects the corrupt Monarchy. The BBC journalist Emily Maitlis allegedly received many plaudits for her "demolition" of Prince Andrew; and yet hordes of critics have pointed out that during the "train-wreck" interview she never once alluded to the crimes of Jimmy Savile which, considering they were sex assaults against under-age females exactly like those attributed to Jeffrey Epstein and Ghislaine Maxwell, seemed like a glaring omission. This is a conscious deception. It's purpose is to confuse the public by making them so uncertain of what all these contemporary political terms mean they will never be able to follow any political debate and hence will not be able to take sides against the establishment. I have seen myself described as a Left-wing Snowflake, a Right-Wing Narcissist and a Liberal Communist, always with the implication that any one of these is an inherently disreputable state-to-be-in, and this is always done with the intention to mislead.

But unfortunately for the super-rich the population have grown so weary of these kinds of games they are now turning away from mainstream media in their droves. The long-running soap operas, news broadcasts, and even major sports like American football are all suffering an inexorable decline in ratings. In spite of the weasel efforts of the highly-paid morning TV presenters much clarity still remains; although it must be said that we could now be enjoying much greater clarity as to what exactly is going on if those who ought to have been the most staunch defenders of Democracy had not betrayed it. As this ongoing adventure has unfolded nothing has sickened me more than the attitude of the rock stars and pop stars and movie stars who were perfectly happy to use Western freedom to get rich but then were unwilling to defend it the moment when it became clear that Western-style Democracy is in peril.

Anyone who could have been a fly on the wall during my journey, and witnessed everything that I have seen, would have been absolutely incensed at the contrast between the legions of poor, working people who have praised my work to the hilt, and the rich and famous people who, to the last man, have fallen over themselves to pretend my work does not even exist. Why would there be such a glaring dichotomy? All around the world people who don't have any money have gone into paroxysms over my film. They have done their best to share it far and wide across social media (millions have had their Facebook accounts closed down by Mark Zuckerberg as a result) and have tried to tell their Internet audience "you will never look at anything in the same way ever again after seeing this movie" so one might reasonably have expected that there might have been just *one* individual amongst those who do have money who shared in this international effusion?

But not a bit of it. Since my movie went viral I have approached Sir Richard Branson, Peter Gabriel, Sting, Alloys Wobben, Steve Hackett, Kevin Godley, Lol Creme, Phil Collins, Gina Rinehart, Tony Banks, Mike Rutherford, Steven Spielberg, George Lucas, Mark Ruffalo, Jeff Skoll, Pierre Omidyar, Rick Wakeman, Duncan Bannatyne, Peter Jones, Enok Groven, Michael Stipe, Lord Melvyn Bragg, Ian Anderson (Jethro Tull) and countless others for financial assistance in getting this picture, which the entire world seems to agree is the single most critically important political Film ever made, into cinemas world wide for the edification and emancipation of the citizens of this entire planet, and they have all declined; even though in most cases they could easily have afforded to. A very bitter pill that I have had to swallow is that when I first tried to tell the world that everything is a rich man's trick even I myself did not know how right I was.

The rich themselves know better than anyone that money equals *power*. You can do pretty much whatever you want if you have lots of it – and you can't get anything done if you have no money at all. This is why the Globalists have been pursuing an ongoing policy of maintaining a V.I.P. Pedophile network for the purposes of sexual blackmail. If any exceptionally talented working class person, like a Paul McCartney or a Billy Connolly, should hit serious pay-dirt and become the sort of arts patron who just might bankroll Films like my own, they make sure he is lured into a 'compromising situation', record the deed with hidden cameras through a two-way mirror, and then take him by the elbow and say "sorry son, you're ours now" And who in this world would risk being a rat against people who had the power to ensure he did life in prison for sexual molestation of a child?

I am not for one moment suggesting that all the illustrious names I have mentioned are guilty of child molestation, in fact it hardly needs stating that most have been much too old for a very long time to contemplate such vigorous activity as sex. Nevertheless I am sure the public must be curious as to why there is always this closing of ranks amongst the very wealthy the moment that the telling of the *entire* truth is placed on the agenda? At the time of going to press all literate people who take an interest in current affairs are sharing amusement at the way in which nefarious Establishment figures like Epstein, Maxwell and most notably Prince Andrew appear to have been caught in their own tangled web. The Trapper trapped as ever. And it has largely been through witnessing this high-level corruption that those same literate people started suggesting that I should bring out my movie in book form. It was their idea, not mine. I myself did not want things to go this way at all. It is a most dispiriting statistic that barely two per cent of the population, regardless of which country one looks at, actually buy and read books.

But at least this little piece of art is now available for the public to purchase. As I have done my best to relate: the elite wouldn't give me any funds; they wouldn't give me any help, they wouldn't agree to any interviews; they wouldn't give me any travel expenses; they wouldn't give me any research grants; they wouldn't give me any commissions, and they have done everything they can to actively prevent distribution. It has taken years of toil, and sweat, and tears, and hare-brained excursions to London to parlay with witless television producers (most of the time using a false name to "stay off the radar") to get this far. Every reader of this book should ask himself what this tells you about the nature of the kind of *laissez-faire* capitalist system we live under? Just as I hope all literate people will think hard on why

Donald Trump, and Joe Biden, nor any other American politician, nor any major American media outlet, whether print, television or film, never ever mentioned my movie even once.

So I hope this little introduction, dear reader, will have given you some useful insight into just how special and unique you yourself are, just because you have taken the trouble to seek out this book. And I hope it's contents will make you fully appreciate the ridiculous lengths the richest people have gone to, and the phenomenal efforts they have made, to stop you from ever finding it or learning the information it contains. As you wander through it's pages never forget that your lords and masters; the people whose faces you never see, and whose names you never hear; who own the jumbo jets and the huge ocean liners and the hotel chains and the gold mines and the big clearing banks – those people would much rather you never had the chance to learn what you are about to find out. Never stop asking yourself why this class of people have done all they can to keep this *book* out of your hands.

– Francis Richard Conolly June 2021

JFK to 9/11, Everything is a Rich Man's Trick

In the immediate aftermath of the assassination of President John F. Kennedy the American government came to the conclusion that a lone gunman had changed the course of human history by killing the most powerful man in the world with three rifle shots fired from the elevated window of an office building.

And for half a century they have stuck rigidly to this fabrication, while critics, scientists, playwrights and poets have produced books, and essays, and films, to prove beyond any shadow of a doubt that this version of our Western history is a physical impossibility.

Over and over again we have been told that this man did it. By himself. He didn't have any help. And he did it because he was a lonely madman, and a Communist to boot. We are also meant to believe that there is nothing remotely suspicious in his being shot, on Live television, in a basement full of police officers, before he had a chance to tell his side of the story. So there is quite clearly no need to investigate further. Of course every thinking person knows this is absolute nonsense, and being nonsensical it naturally leads thinking people to ask some very important questions like; why did the American government come up with such a lame and improbable scenario to account for what had happened?

And then why did they stick with it so dogmatically for so many years afterwards?

Exactly what, and who, are they protecting?

And how can it be that even such venerable institutions as the BBC have played along with this charade in the intervening decades?

We now know that there were actually eight riflemen firing at the President on that day.

We know where they were located in Dealey Plaza: and, we know their names.

However, those with sharp eyes will already be asking themselves why we are only showing the location of six assassins in this schematic?

We're doing this because any casual onlooker who happened to be in Dealey Plaza at 12:29 on November 22nd 1963 might well have caught sight of these six.

Many people did. Witnesses like Arnold Rowland; Richard Randolph Carr; Lee Bowers; Amos Euins; Mary Moorman; they all gave precise descriptions of men they observed in the windows of the Book Depository, and on the famous grassy knoll.

But none of them observed two of the riflemen who shot at the President, no one did.

And the reason why no one did is itself the key to the mystery. A mystery which begins with a very simple question.

Supposing you wanted to shoot at a man on a barren empty street without anybody seeing you? Where could you possibly hide?

However the rifleman who took part in the assassination were not as important to an understanding of what the Kennedy assassination was really all about as were a group of twenty men who had gathered together the night before at the home of Dallas oil millionaire Clint Murchison.

These men were a much more important part of the story than the assassins themselves, because they hired the eight snipers, and paid them.

We even know how much they paid them.

So who were these men? what brought them together to orchestrate such a foul and despicable deed? why did they, and more importantly, those who came after them cover-up the crime with such ruthless brutality for so long afterwards? And how can it be that these men, and what they stood for, has left an indelible legacy which still influences our daily lives right up to the present day?

To answer these questions we must, inevitably, step back into history, and most people will not like this very much, because most people have very little interest in history.

Butch Cassidy and the Sundance Kid
BUTCH: Open the door or that's it! You think E.H. Harriman would get himself killed for you? Woodcock?
WOODCOCK: I work for Mr. E.H. Harriman of the Union Pacific Railroad! And he entrusted me!

This however is going to be a history lesson quite unlike anything that anyone has ever heard.

It certainly will be nothing like what we are taught in school; and yet it begins with a name which most people have heard but probably won't be able to place.

The name of E.H. Harriman. Who was E.H. Harriman?

I'm sure Americans in particular will be amused to learn that Edward Henry Harriman was actually a real historical figure; this man was one of America's first industrial giants, and like the Rockefellers

in oil, and the Carnegies in steel, he got his start by borrowing money from the Rothschilds, of whom we'll hear more later, to create a monopoly for his own business, which was railroads. He was the nineteenth-century railroad king. It was a monopoly which wouldn't be allowed today, and it helped in turn to create the Rockefeller oil monopoly.

Now this gave America's first industrial giants colossal power. These were the first people in human history, we mustn't forget, whose businesses were worth more than

most countries; people whose fortunes dwarfed anything that the Caesars or the Tudors or the Medici ever dreamed of.

So being greedy they used this power to engage in price-fixing. Naturally. They formed a cartel.

Their attitude was that they could charge whatever they liked for steel and oil and transporting goods on the railways.

They knew that all American business was dependent on them, and they'd made sure there was no competition, so they could ignore market forces and charge pretty much whatever they liked.

Now this naturally caused resentment and it's very interesting that the press at that time started calling these first Illuminati bankers and industrialists "Robber Barons"

Of course once these fortunes began to be made others naturally tried to get in on the act. One who succeeded was JP Morgan, who became a private banker during this period; but modern critics have discovered that far from being the richest man in America everyone thought he was, it turned out upon his death that Morgan actually only owned 17% of Morgan Bank, and that like so many others he was simply a front for the Rothschild family.

Five years after E.H. Harriman died and handed on the business to his sons W. Averill Harriman and E. Roland (Bunny) Harriman, this new breed of Western business moguls faced their first really big test with the coming of World War One.

Once again, we must never forget that this was the first time in human history that a truly global conflict had been fought. It was sure to have long-lasting international repercussions, and many observers at the time had their doubts as to whether western industrial capitalism, which was still in its infancy, could cope with the demands of war production.

In the world economic recession which followed many feared these fledgling industries might vanish altogether as countries struggled with debt and war reparations.

But actually Western capitalism emerged from World War one in a far stronger state than it was in at the beginning. So how could this be?

The first world war taught the new class of international bankers and industrialists a very simple lesson: war is good for business.

Take, for instance, Remington. We tend to associate their name with typewriters, but actually they made most of the rifles and handguns used during the Great War, and made a colossal fortune in the process.

The Banks, in their turn, lapped this up, because it meant that Defence contractors were having no trouble repaying the huge loans they had outstanding and, best of all, the world's richest nations had had to borrow huge sums from the merchant bankers in the first place to finance the war – the Americans and the British just as much as the Germans; and they would now be repaying these loans to the Banks for decades to come at a steep rate of interest.

For international merchant bankers, the Rothschilds in particular, the First World War had been a gift from Heaven; and people watching this should ask themselves a simple question before passing judgement.

Supposing you were in business during that war? And the contract you had with the government to supply the troops with tin hats, or boots, or uniforms, or gunpowder was netting *you* millions every year in profit; and then one day the war ended? And your money stopped: completely?

What do you think your attitude to war might be?

That war was good for business was not the only lesson the ruling classes learned during this period.

The Russian Revolution of 1917 terrified rich people all over the world.

Watching Lenin and Trotsky taking over such a vast area of the globe the Kings and Queens of Europe's tiny sovereign states in particular became extremely nervous.

The question on all their minds was: supposing the Communist success in Russia should inspire their own working class to rise in revolt?

Many of the crowned heads of Europe, like England's George V, had been related to Tsar Nicholas, and the brutal execution of the Tsar and his family, particularly the bayoneting of his young daughters, sent a shock wave through the upper classes of every nation.

Did a similar fate lie in store for the royal families of Holland, Sweden, Spain and England?

This question was lying heavily on the thoughts of the elite when the first world war ended in 1918 and it had the effect of focusing the minds of the new Illuminati bankers and industrialists on the question of what to do for best with a defeated and dilapidated Germany?

The population were poor, penniless and worn out, yet the German economy still contained some of the most sophisticated and expensive industrial stock on the planet.

The Illuminati sensed an opportunity.

Supposing, as the world's first international businessmen, they could get their hands on Germany's steel mills? Her coal mines? Her factories, ports, and her shipbuilding industry?

Over the years certain names have become very familiar to those who maintain an interest in the Kennedy assassination – none more so than Allen Dulles, whom Kennedy fired after the Bay of Pigs disaster. And yet later he somehow managed to chair the Warren Commission which was supposed to be investigating Kennedy's death.

Something few people know however, is that Dulles and his older brother John Foster Dulles wrote the Treaty of Versailles.

They were both lawyers of Sullivan & Cromwell, and it was largely they who decided that the German people must pay war reparations totalling 135 billion marks: a mind-boggling sum at that time, which today translates into two hundred and fifty Trillion.

When this was announced the legendary UK economist J. Maynard Keynes maintained it was a ludicrous sum, and he did a swift calculation from which he reasoned that it would take Germany until 1988 – sixty years hard labour, to pay it off.

But it didn't. So, why?

Maynard-Keynes sensed that the Dulles brothers, backed as they were by the new Illuminati, were trying quite deliberately to sabotage the German economy, and they succeeded.

As mass unemployment led to hyperinflation the famous stories of people papering their walls with worthless Reichmarks, and handing over their life savings for a loaf of bread, soon followed.

With German investors on their knees the new Illuminati moved in, and began buying up shares of stock in German industry at a knockdown price.

Now why did they do this? The cynical mind would say, to make a buck, but it really wasn't that simple. What they wanted was to make Germany strong again, so that she would become a bulwark against Soviet Communism.

It was around this time that the newspapers which these same rich people owned made sure the word "Bolshy" a truncation of "Bolshevik" entered the English language, so that we would associate Bolshevism with aggression; and it was with these subtle and not-so-subtle methods that the International elite began to shape our destiny for the remainder of the 20th Century.

Intellectuals of the period were furious; they were incensed; they were depressed; and you get a very good feeling of the political atmosphere of the time from the diaries of the Labour politician Harold Nicholson when he writes:

Extract from *Judgement at Nuremberg*
EMIL HAHN: Germany was fighting for its life. Certain measures were needed to protect it from its enemies. I cannot say that I am sorry we applied those measures. We were a Bulwark against Bolshevism. We were a pillar of Western culture. A Bulwark and a pillar the West may yet wish to retain.

We have lost our willpower, since our willpower is divided. The people of the governing class think only of their own fortunes, which means hatred of the Reds. Our class interests cut across our national interests and I go to bed in gloom.

With such heavy investment coming into the country, particularly from America and Britain, Germany began to recover very rapidly. And then the new class of international financiers began searching around for a homegrown authoritarian political movement they could support. What they needed was someone they could count on to be both aggressive and expansionist.

Ultra right-wing causes, which at normal times would have been ignored and marginalized, were suddenly given very careful consideration, until finally the rich elite found a man, and an idea, which they felt might deliver the political outcome they desired.

Adolf Hitler. And his fledgling National Socialist Party.

At the same time that the world's rich elite began grooming Hitler for his starring role they also became even more deeply involved in military

Adolf Hitler, Emil Maurice, Hermann Kriebel, Rudolf Hess, and Friedrich Weber at Landsberg Prison

intelligence. I say even more because the Dulles brothers, Averill Harriman, and the chief of Rockefeller-owned Remington, Samuel F. Pryor, a man referred to as the original merchant of death, had a relationship with American military intelligence stretching back into World War one – the lesson here being that the American variant of military intelligence started out with businessmen protecting their investments: just as if they were a Mafia.

Right from the very beginning it had nothing to do with national security, and everything to do with money.

In Hitler the Illuminati had found a ready-made stooge who could be the face of this autocratic new movement.

And when the time came to put together a new Secret Intelligence Service which was going to help protect all the money they had tied up in the German economy these men also found one was readily available – the Order of Skull & Bones at Yale University.

Discussion of secret societies is something of a minefield, because it so easily invites ridicule. It is very difficult for the general public to accept that the super-rich leaders of their Western world can possibly be as mad and deranged as they actually are.

The public, generally speaking, are sensible and level-headed people who have to balance their cheque-books, so they inevitably tend to laugh at stories about Satanists and Occult believers. But if you talk to any well-informed historians they are all aware of the important role which various secret societies have played in human history. The Black Hand always played a pivotal role in the history of the Mafia. If you talk to anyone in the UK who is political, and reads books, they are always aware that the ruling class of Britain, including every member of the royal family, is a Freemason, and the emblem of the Death's Head was sported on the caps of the high-ranking Nazi officers from the very beginning.

The symbols of these secret societies always seem to play around with some kind of Skull and Bones motif; so that it's abundantly clear what their mission statement is – these people are pirates; willing to commit any crime for big money. And they first became established in America at Yale College in 1832 with General William Huntington Russell and Alphonso Taft.

Of course being a secret society they made other people curious about them, and in 1867 some undergraduates from a rival campus Society broke into their headquarters to see what this Skull & Bones thing was all about.

They reported that inside there were lots of Lamps and Candles; many dilapidated human skulls, lying next to a Fool's cap and bells; and it was morbidly dark because the walls were covered in black velvet.

Having established a suitably satanic atmosphere initiation rites were then performed on new members, who had to engage in group masturbation and sodomy while they lay in a coffin.

Now it's very easy to dismiss all of this as bizarre, silly and irrelevant until you see the list of Skull and Bones members who have ruled America since Skull and Bones began.

Although they only graduate 15 initiates a year those 15 have always gone on to occupy the very highest positions in American society.

U.S. Secretary of State William Max Evarts was a Bonesman; as was Treasury Secretary Franklin McVeigh; State of Connecticut Chief Justice Simeon Eden Baldwin, and the 27th President of the United States William Howard Taft.

The founder of American football, Walter Camp, came through Skull and Bones, as did the very first chairman of the Federal Reserve Pierre Jay, and director of Remington Arms and many other corporations, Percy Rockefeller.

Averill Harriman the son of E.H. Harriman and founder of W.A. Harriman & Co., one of the largest investment banks in the world, was a Bonesman, and so were both of the Bush U.S. Presidents, George H.W. and George W.

During his Presidency John F. Kennedy was surrounded by Bonesmen, like McGeorge Bundy, and David Acheson, son of Dean Acheson. Kennedy knew these men refer to each other as "brothers under the skin." They swear an oath of secrecy and then ruthlessly vow to help each other's careers in any way they can throughout their lives, even if it means committing murder.

In Britain every literate person knows that all of the top police officers are Freemasons, because if there are 10 candidates for a top job a Mason will always select a brother Mason for the post.

Skull and Bones works the same way; and JFK took this problem so seriously that he even made speeches warning America about the danger of secret societies.

He knew the people on this list were neither silly nor irrelevant; because he knew they were the real holders of power in America: operating, as they were, as an un-elected shadow government accountable to no-one.

And it was these same people who brought Hitler to power during the 1920's by becoming business partners with leading German industrialists. The reality of the situation prevailing at that time can be very easily understood simply by looking at the cover of a Spanish edition of Fritz Thyssen's book "I Paid Hitler" on which he is depicted as a puppet master controlling Hitler's strings.

After the war, Thyssen "denied authorship" of *I Paid for Hitler*

Thyssen was a billionaire industrialist. He was the man who built up the Bismarck. His company, United Steel Works, made three quarters of all Germany's steel, and he joined together with Skull and Bones member Prescott Bush and his father-in-law George Herbert Walker to financially assist the Nazi Party.

Together they recruited head of the German Central Bank, Hjalmar Schact, to the Fascist cause, and

then combined with other leading industrialists to sign the letter which convinced German president Hindenburg to appoint Hitler as Chancellor on the 20th of February 1933. Had anyone inquired around this time about the postal address of the Nazi Party they could legitimately have been told that it was 39 Broadway, Manhattan, New York. Because this was where Averill Harriman, Prescott Bush and George Herbert Walker kept their office and being no fool Fritz Thyssen used their Banking services to set up secret cash funds funnelled through another Bank, the Bank Voor Handel en Scheepvaart, to finance the building of the first official Nazi Party headquarters, the Brown House.

This was all done with the full cooperation of the Dutch bankers who orchestrated this entire sinister business with the assistance of the Thyssen family Lawyer, Allen Dulles.

Of course the Germans themselves were ecstatic. We've all seen the newsreels from that time in which they are stomping around in their jackboots acting like a master race because they had swallowed the propaganda that they were being led to glory by a superman who had rebuilt the economy and Germany's infrastructure all by himself.

This was a lie. Hitler didn't have any money. You can only build autobahns with one thing – capital investment, and that investment came mainly from America.

The Nazis were also given a lot of help from the city of London; help which came mainly in the shape of Sir Montague Collet Norman, the Governor of the Bank of England.

Norman was connected to Bush and Walker through the merger of Harriman's with the Brown Brothers, who traded in London as Brown/Shipley; hence, Brown Brothers Harriman.

The people behind this multinational investment bank had a long-standing racial tradition. Few British people at the time were aware that they only enjoyed relatively cheap clothing because it was all made from slave cotton brought from America on the Brown Brothers ships and sold to British Mill owners.

Montagu Norman was heir to this colossal Brown Brothers fortune. As the *de facto* head of world banking he made no secret of his only being interested in the richest 1% of people; and even as the newspapers began to fill with stories of Nazi concentration camps he still declared himself to be Hitler's most avid supporter.

"We must lend Nazi Germany 90 million marks" he declared.

"It may never be repaid but it will be less of a loss than the fall of Nazism"

One might have thought Sir Montague's close personal friends the royal family would have been outraged by his comments. Nothing could be further from the truth.

It is part of the remit of this book to try and make people aware of the tricks the rich play in order to control how we think.

George Orwell once said that the ruling class in every age have tried to impose a false view of the world upon their followers, and there's no better example than the way in which the British have been duped into believing that their Royal family are called Windsor; and descend from English kings like Henry VIII.

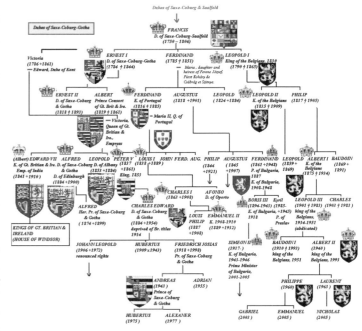

The British royal family are actually German, and their real name is Saxe-Coburg-Gotha. They only changed it to Windsor (after Windsor Castle) in 1917 to hide the fact that they were German during the First World War.

Prince Harry, in honour of his German roots, has been known to dress as a Nazi on several occasions.

Dozens of critics have pointed out that the Duke of Edinburgh's Brother-in-law was the head of the Nazi SS: and King Edward VIII, before he abdicated to marry the American divorcee Wallis Simpson visited Hitler to make it abundantly clear to the whole world that he too was a Nazi.

He even signed his name Hertzog von Windsor.

Thinking people during this period realized that this whole thing with kissing-up to the Fuhrer somehow transcended national boundaries. The rich people from the most diverse countries had bonded together because they all shared a common goal.

The kings and the queens and the international bankers and industrialists wanted to make certain communism could never succeed. They were determined they weren't going to finish up like the Russian royal family; and they were determined to hang on to their money.

They were much more afraid of the ordinary working people in their own countries than they were of Fascist Germany, and this prevailing sentiment amongst the world's ruling class led America's elite to attempt a Fascist coup d'etat in 1934.

I hope it will be plain to people by now that Hitler's economic miracle is the greatest myth in human history. There was no economic miracle. There are no miracles – and if there are, *why can't the Germans do it all again now?*

If you want to construct a network of new roads and new steelworks and new factories you need one thing. Money. You need investment.

And the investment didn't come from Hitler, it came from Brown Brothers Harriman, and their business associate Fritz Thyssen.

It came from Hjalmar Schact, and his best friend Sir Montague Collet Norman. It came from men like Axel Wenner-Gren, the Swedish multi-millionaire arms manufacturer, and Charles Bedaux the French business mogul.

These people were all in the same bed with their Nazi friends, the Duke and Duchess of Windsor, the Dulles brothers, Prescott Sheldon Bush, and George Herbert Walker with whom they'd created the Union Bank for laundering Nazi money, and with stage one of their plan for world domination complete they now turned to the second phase, which was meant to be the overthrow of American democracy, and the imposition of Fascist government upon the United States.

In order to pull this off these Nazis raised money from America's richest families; many of whom, in this new consumerist society had become household names – the Colgate family; the Birdseye family; the Du Pont family, the Rockefeller family.

These people handed over millions to the American Financiers of Hitler so they could hire, train and supply a private army which would attempt to overthrow the democratically elected government of Franklin Delano Roosevelt, and impose Fascist dictatorship in America. Of course it's natural to wonder, considering they had such advantages, how on earth they failed to pull it off?

The simple answer is that they chose the wrong man.

Because their choice to lead this Nazi insurrection was Major General Smedley Darlington Butler; the most decorated soldier of the period and in all of American history perhaps the most unsung hero of all.

Because Smedley Butler was the most genuine Democrat and lover of Liberty the world has ever seen.

Smedley Butler address to the nation
I appeared before the congressional committee, the highest representation of the American people, under subpoena to tell what I knew of activities which I believe might lead to an attempt to set up a fascist dictatorship. The plan as outlined to me was to form an organization of veterans to use as a bluff or as a club at least to intimidate the government and break down our democratic institutions. The upshot of the whole thing was that I was supposed to lead an organization of 500,000 men which would be able to take over the functions of government. My main interest in all this is to preserve our democratic institutions. I want to retain the right to vote, the right to speak freely and the right to write. If we maintain these basic principles our democracy is safe. No dictatorship can exist with suffrage, freedom of speech and press."

Smedley Butler tricked the plotters into thinking he was interested for just long enough until he was sure who all the major players were, and then he told the President.

This put FDR in a quite impossible position.

America at that time was just coming out of the Great Depression. The last thing he wanted was to cause another economic downturn, and he feared that if he scooped up all the leading bankers and captains of industry in the United States and threw them all in jail the country just might fall apart. So what could he do?

To Smedley Butler's utter incredulity he chose in the end to do nothing. In spite of the fact that these men had committed treason and should have been hanged, their power was such that they were not even charged, let alone tried, and so great was their influence they were able to keep America out of the war until 8 o'clock in the morning on December the 7th 1941.

With the Japanese attack on Pearl Harbour Roosevelt finally realized he had to do something. His response was the "Trading with the Enemy Act" which allowed him to seize assets like the Union Bank through which Bush, Walker and Harriman had been financing Thyssen.

Roosevelt didn't realize however, that it was already a case of too little too late; because without his knowledge American business moguls had been tumbling over one another for two years in their efforts to assist, and do business with, the Hitler regime.

Typical of this American "spirit of enterprise" was Sosthenes Bhen, the president of AT&T, who flew immediately to Berlin when war was declared to put in Hitler's phone lines.

He gave the Nazis the most high-tech state-of-the-art telecommunications system in the world at that time so that Hitler could rule the European mainland with the maximum efficiency.

Rich men have been hiring thugs to do their dirty work, especially to frighten people, since human civilization began. What people have to try to appreciate is that Nazism in reality was simply the first time in human history that the rich had enough wealth to hire an entire country of thugs to do their dirty work.

Clarence Birdseye

Samuel B. Colgate

Irénée du Pont, Jr

David Rockefeller

Some of the most emotive images in world history are those of the Nazi war machine sweeping across the Low Countries to begin their occupation of France, and people have always assumed that the trucks used for the miles-long troop convoys must have been German trucks.

But if anyone at that time had taken the trouble to lift up the cowling, and look at the engine, they would have found these were actually Ford trucks, which had been built with personal permission from Henry Ford who was sitting in his office 4,000 miles away in Dearborn Michigan: a service for which he was given the Grand Cross of the Eagle, the highest honour the Nazis ever bestowed on a civilian.

Hitler so admired Henry Ford he kept a life-sized portrait of him on the wall next to his desk, and even his legendary Panzer Tanks were tainted by these sorts of practices, because they were made by I.G. Farben who had entered into a cartel with the Rockefeller's Standard Oil.

The government in Washington knew all about this and largely did nothing. Licensing arrangements for trading with the enemy in wartime were issued without any fuss, even to the extent that after the occupation of France the Chase & Morgan Banks in Paris simply carried on doing business as usual.

From David Rovics "Live at Club Passim" CD
Ford sued the U.S. Army, the U.S. government, in the 1950s because during the war the U.S. Air Force bombed their tank making facilities in Germany. This is true! In what was it? like 52 or something? they sued the U.S. government for destroying their factories and they won! They won the lawsuit! So I had to write a little song for Henry here:

Ford built tanks for the Nazis,
And Nazis used those tanks
To gun down lots of soldiers
In the U.S. Army ranks.
Yes, Henry Ford was a Fascist!
And a nasty one was he!
He built tanks for anyone
For the proper fee…

I.G. Farben headquarters

The incredible truth, which the rich elite have managed to hide from the world for seventy years through their control over schoolbooks and our education system, is that the Nazi war machine was actually an American business; and for the Rockefeller's, Du Pont's, Harriman's, Walkers and Bushes in particular it was a highly lucrative business.

33

For their part Coca Cola's contribution to the war effort was to sell Billions of soft drinks to the thirsty Nazis while they were strafing and bombing Allied soldiers – particularly in very hot regions. In the desert, where refrigerators tend to be scarce, there were even stories of Messerschmitt pilots wrapping wet towels around bottles of coke, tying them to their aircraft, then flying up to altitude where the cold and the wind-chill turned the wet towel into a solid block of ice. They would then dive down, crack open the towel, and enjoy an ice-cold coke in the Desert!

If they had wanted to the Western multinationals could have grounded the Luftwaffe and stopped the war at any time, because the German aircraft were totally dependent on imported supplies of tetra-ethyl Lead, an additive which prevents knocking in aero engines, but Standard Oil kept the supply of this vital resource going through neutral Switzerland for the entire war.

And any Dutch people who might be wondering at this point what kind of percentage the Swiss took from this little arrangement? They need to be aware that thanks to Prince Bernhard von Lippi of the Netherlands, the father of the recently retired Queen Beatrix and prominent member of the Nazi Party, Royal Dutch Shell gave Hitler millions of tonnes of crude oil for nothing.

The Dutch royal family actually fuelled the invasion force which annexed Holland, and were instrumental in helping the Nazis to rape their own country.

But most shocking of all is the truth of what really happened in the little Polish town of Oswiecim.

This sleepy little hamlet just happened to be in an extremely mineral-rich region, particularly for coal,

which Western industrialists had wanted to get their hands on for years. With the coming of the Hitler regime and the invasion of Poland the Fascist financiers had the bright idea of turning this conquered region into an investors paradise by building a Nazi concentration camp near the town and utilizing the slave labour available to drastically reduce their own production costs.

Few people are aware of the gigantic scale of the Nazi concentration camp Network and are blissfully unaware that the real purpose behind their construction was to make a profit for the rich; which is why they stole all the Gold Watches, Gold wedding rings and Gold teeth fillings and melted them down into Gold ingots.

To this day there are bars of Gold lying in the vaults of the Bank of England which have the Nazi swastika stamped on them; Gold stolen from Jewish corpses.

It shouldn't come as any great surprise that George Herbert Walker's family were slave owners on the cotton plantations of 1930's America.

Walker was used to organizing slave labour; so while his business associate Averill Harriman was paying for Hitler's half-million SS troops and supplying them all with brand-new Thompson sub-machine guns, because he did, Walker took over the management of this new Polish concentration camp; and when his Nazi friends started complaining that they couldn't pronounce the name 'Oswiecim' any better than I can, they all got together and decided they had better germanize the name into something which sat more comfortably on Nazi tongues.

It was in this way that the world first heard of Auschwitz.

Because the truth about Auschwitz and the entire Nazi war machine is that they were essentially no different to McDonald's – they were American business enterprises abroad; businesses which the richest European families invested in, and businesses which, because of slave labour, made obscene profits which Prescott Sheldon Bush took and placed in a blind trust which later financed a Bush political dynasty which produced two Presidents of the United States: his son, George Herbert Walker Bush, and his grandson, George Walker Bush.

This picture of the railway leading into Auschwitz has, since world war two,

become the iconic image of the Holocaust. To us it now represents something like the gate to Hell; but how differently, one wonders, would we have looked at this image all of our lives? if we had always known that this railway line was an American Railway line, laid by the Harriman Brothers on behalf of Uncle Sam?

The Standard Oil/I.G. Farben cartel even made the Zyklon B gas for the Jewish Holocaust.

Now anyone who at this point is thinking that all this simply cannot be true because if it was someone would have sued? Well someone did.

This information came into the public domain because of a Dutch intelligence agent who was so disgusted when he found all of this out he leaked it to the press, as a result of which two very senior Jewish gentlemen, Kurt Julius Goldstein and Peter Gingold filed suit against the American government.

Of course the more discriminating among us will now be asking how it can be that this story went completely unreported in the mainstream media? One might just as well ask why *The Times* in London was writing favourable stories about the Nazi concentration camps throughout the 1930's? and why Lord Rothmere was still referring to Hitler as 'a great gentleman' as late as 1940? you really would think by now that people would have realized that it isn't so much the bias in the media which really matters, it's the things they know about but never tell you that really matter.

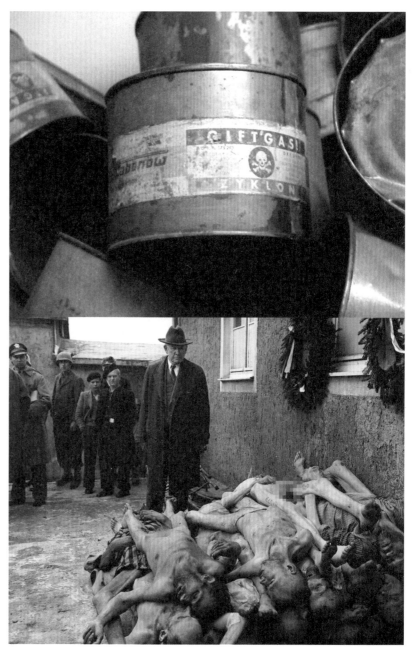

Extract from *Judgement At Nuremberg*

HANS ROLFE: Where is the responsibility of the Vatican who signed in 1933 the Concordat with Hitler giving him his first tremendous prestige?

Are we now to find the Vatican guilty?

Where is the responsibility of the world leader Winston Churchill? who said in an open letter to the *London Times* in 1938.. 1938! your honour! Were England to suffer national disaster they should pray to God to send a man of the strength of mind and will of an Adolf Hitler.

Are we now to find Winston Churchill guilty?

Where is the responsibility of those American industrialists who helped Hitler to rebuild his Armaments??! And profited by that rebuilding!!

Are we now to find the American industrialists guilty?!!

No! your honour! No!

Germany alone is not guilty!

The whole world is as responsible for Hitler as Germany!

It is an easy thing to condemn one man in the dock. It is an easy thing to condemn the German people! To speak of the basic flaw in the German character which allowed Hitler to rise to power!

But at the same time comfortably to ignore the basic flaw of character which made the Russians sign pacts with him!! Winston Churchill praise him!!

AMERICAN INDUSTRIALISTS PROFIT BY HIM!!!

Because the truth is that the press knew exactly what was going on in the concentration camps all through the war.

They never said a word about it because they knew who was making money from the slave labour.

Now it's very easy to imagine what the response of a conservative politician, American or British, would be to all of this.

If all of this is true he's about to ask why nobody said a word about American industrialists building Hitler's war machine at the Nuremberg trials?

How come it never got mentioned?

In school were are taught that the Allies defeated Nazi Germany in World War Two. This is not true.

The Nazis won the war.

Because the real Nazis. The Rich. Played on both sides.

That is what a rich businessman does. He arranges things so that he is well thought of by both sides, so then whoever wins, he wins, and his money is safe.

Now a lot of people will still think it is simply ludicrous to suggest the Second World War was a phoney war. They are bound to say that no-one who was there at the time thought it was a phoney war. Really??

Now obviously the British and the Dutch in particular will have a very hard time accepting that their royal family profited from Nazi concentration camp slave labour: but if you go online, there is so much about this on the Internet now. It's become plain that historians are more and more proving that those days were really all about the Western world's rich coming together to fund a Nazi war machine which was meant to protect *them* from the Soviets.

The Duke of Edinburgh practically admitted this when he said:

"In those days we were anti-communist because the Russians killed half my bloody family!"

And when this cabal of secret Nazis got together to discuss how they were going to pay for this Nazi war machine; because rich people never accept a loss, they hired a psychopath, Hitler, who they knew would go along with their building concentration camps so that slave labour would pay for all the planes and the tanks and the guns, and you can see in the more intelligent movies from that period, like Hitchcock's *Saboteur* that the artists and writers of that time knew the rich were Fascist, and completely understood what they were really up to.

Extract from the movie *Dunkirk*

FOREMAN: A new baby. 200 gross of Buckles. Unlimited petrol. And all the Whiskey you want. You're sitting pretty aren't you Holden? Yes it is a lovely war.

HOLDEN: Well wouldn't you if you were in my place? Wouldn't everybody? Doesn't everybody? The war's a blasted phoney anyway.

ANGRY SEAMAN: I'm a bit tired of that!

HOLDEN: Tired of what?

ANGRY SEAMAN: This phoney war business!

HOLDEN: Well isn't it?

ANGRY SEAMAN: No! it's not! I've just come out of hospital after 10 days in an open boat off the Faroes and I'm sick and tired of Blokes like you with soft jobs ashore! come outside!

FOREMAN: Now don't be silly.

ANGRY SEAMAN: I've lost two fingers off that hand! but I'm going take you outside and knock your block off with my right!

BARMAN: Hey take it easy! there's no need for that!

HOLDEN: I'm sorry. I apologize. I'll come outside if you insist.

FOREMAN: That won't do any good. It's not his fault. It's the fault of all of us.

ANGRY SEAMAN: You make me sick! all of you! It may be a phoney war to you but it's not to all the boys at sea! never has been!

Extract from the 1942 movie *Saboteur*

KANE: Why is it that you sneer every time you refer to this country? you've done pretty well here, I don't get it? TOBIN No you wouldn't, you're one of the ardent believers; the good American. Oh there are millions like you; people that plod along without asking questions. I hate to use the word stupid but it seems to be the only one that applies. The great masses.... The moron millions.... Well there are a few of us who are unwilling to just troop along. A few of us who are clever enough to see that there's much more to be done than just live small, complacent lives. A few of us in America who desire a more profitable type of government. When you think about it Mister Kane, the competence of Totalitarian nations is much higher than ours. They get things done. KANE Yeah. They get things done. They bomb cities. Sink ships. Torture and murder so you and your friends can eat off of gold plate. It's a great philosophy. TOBIN I neither intend to be bombed nor sunk Mister Kane; that's why I'm leaving now. And if things don't go right for you, if we should win, then I'll come back. Perhaps I can get what I want then. Power. Yes. I want that as much as you want your comfort; or your job, or that girl. We all have different tastes as you can see. Only I'm willing to back my tastes with the necessary force.

Where was the Mafia while all this was going on?

Well a great deal which historians have learned recently, especially from sources like *Double-Cross*, the book written by Sam Giancana's brother, has made it clear that the Mafia was much the same as the so-called German economic miracle, and the American financed Nazi war machine and concentration camps.

The mob in reality was a very different animal from the one portrayed by the movies and the media.

American feature films have tended to focus on the exploits of gangsters like Richard Cain the famous crime-busting Chicago cop who was planted in the police force to be a spy for Giancana, and hoods like Charles Nicoletti and Milwaukee Phil Alderisio two of his favourite hit men who built they're own hit-mobile so they could shoot people from the back of a moving car.

Amongst many other atrocities this pair committed was one in which they forced the head of Billy McCarthy into a vice and squeezed until his eyeball popped out: an incident which a certain American Film director felt was so entertaining he included it in one of his movies. What most people have failed to realise however is that in most cases the Mafia Chieftains who actually ran

Richard Cain

Charles Nicoletti

Phil Alderisio

organized crime did not approve, generally speaking, of these acts of gross brutality. Not that they gave a damn about morals, but the cleverest amongst them, like Paul "the Waiter" Ricca, realized that sensationalized events like the St. Valentine's Day Massacre produce public outrage, and a crackdown on their illegal activities.

Rica realized that the effectiveness of mobsters like Diamond Joe Esposito came from keeping a low profile; and it was the Mafia bosses who learned this lesson best; Santos Trafficante and Sam Giancana in particular, who in later years became the most successful.

Even today few Americans appreciate the extent to which their country was being controlled by organized crime in the 1930's. The mob were in total control of

Extract from *The Godfather*
(Featuring Leonardo Passafaro who few people know was a real Mafia hit-man) LUCA BRASI: Don Corleone. I am honoured and grateful that you have invited me to your daughter's wedding … (embarrassing pause) on the day of your daughter's wedding.

Hollywood because all the union labour needed to make Films; carpenters, set construction, catering, they were all under the control of the mob. In particular the control of the Teamsters union: the drivers and haulage people who made essential deliveries to absolutely everyone, meant that virtually all American business was caught in the web of Mafia racketeering.

Studio bosses like Harry Cohn, Louis B. Meyer and the Warner Brothers knew they had to play along to get anything done at all. The big studio heads, like all rich businessmen, found they were forced to become friends with Mafia dons, and the individual who exploited this situation most effectively was a gangster few people have ever heard of. Murray "the Camel" Humphreys.

Generally speaking the ethnically Italian gangsters of this period were coarse, brutal and most importantly ignorant men. They had no education. They couldn't hold an intelligent conversation because they'd spent no time in school.

This made doing business with refined and sophisticated entrepreneurs difficult – not to say embarrassing, and Sam Giancana was quick to spot this.

So, whenever a business deal needed to be made by someone with style and sophistication, he would send along his silver-tongued Welshman, Murray "the Camel," so-called because he was known for being sartorial, and for cutting a dash in expensive Camel-hair coats.

Humphreys became a crucial figure during the pre-war period because his contact with the luminaries of Hollywood meant he received invitations from senior politicians who wanted to rub shoulders with stars like Clark Gable, George Raft, Cary Grant, Gary Cooper, Marilyn Monroe, and Frank Sinatra all of whom were Mafia-controlled, and used by the mob as bag-men moving colossal sums of money around the country; because Giancana cynically realized the authorities were too star-struck to ever check their luggage.

He even used a priest for the same purpose who he referred to as "Father Cash" and just as the priest was happy to take his percentage, so the politicians, who Giancana always maintained were the easiest to corrupt, were happy to do the same.

In Esposito's time he had boasted of buying votes for Calvin Coolidge.

By the time of World War two Sam Giancana was boasting to his younger brother "we own the White House."

He was adamant that every state governor, congressman, and senior judge in the country was on the take, and the mob's most spectacular success, as they sought control over all the big players, was their corrupting of FBI director J. Edgar Hoover.

It's become fairly widely known in recent years that Hoover was a transvestite homosexual: what is less well-known is the elaborate scheme he dreamed up for accepting Mafia bribes. What he used to do was to go to the two-dollar window at the racetrack where he was photographed many times by the press to give himself a clean upstanding image.

J. Edgar Hoove

Frank Costello

Clyde Tolson and J. Edgar Hoover

What the Pressmen didn't know was that he always took along a crooked emissary, who placed huge bets which ran into the thousands at another window on races which were fixed by the mob boss Frank Costello.

By keeping Hoover supplied with millions in winnings, and holding on to compromising photographs of the FBI chief having sex with his lover Clyde Tolson, which several CIA agents claim they've seen, the Mafia had American law enforcement entirely under their control.

So the question then is what do you do with that kind of power? The answer is that when you're the American Mafia you routinely wipe out what they call do-gooders. This is how organized crime has influenced American society for nearly a century.

If a decent man becomes a rising star in politics and looks as if he might try to make a better life for ordinary people they simply kill him as a matter of routine; and in the book they wrote together Chuck and Sam Giancana Jr., are at pains to point out that a classic early case of this practice was the assassination of Anton Cermak.

Cermak was a democratic politician who had tried to crack down on Al Capone's bootlegging operations. Many felt he would go on to become a great President himself until he was shot while on stage with FDR by Guiseppe Zangara. After the murder Zangara claimed it was a political act, and he ought to be entitled to clemency because he simply hated all rich people.

But this was actually what he'd simply been told to say by the mob, who were using him as a fall-guy.

When he went to the electric chair Sam Giancana turned to his brother and expressed his

Anton Cermak

Guiseppe Zangara

pleasure and how 'nice and neat' the whole affair had been, and he further explained that choosing a patsy to wipe out a politician who was a do-gooder was something the Italian Mafia "had been doing forever."

It was a practice "as old as the Sicilian Hills" and he was amazed at how the Mafia kept getting away with it, because "you really would think people would catch on."

1. This was 1935.
2. You have a decent chief executive
3. Murdered in broad daylight.
4. Shot, by a patsy.
5. Who is later killed himself by the authorities. Does this sound familiar?

However even in Cermak's time the mob could not be said to be in complete control of American life because while they controlled the streets through their influence over politics and the justice system they were not yet in control of the United States military or its mainstream media.

Tragically this all started to change with a series of events which began with the scuttling of the *SS Normandie* by a Manhattan-based Nazi agent.

This was February the 9th 1942, and having just joined the war the United States was trying to keep its allies supplied with vital war material using convoys which were loaded on the waterfront and sailed almost every day out of New York Harbour.

As everyone knows many fell prey to the wolf packs of German u-boats, and the *Normandie* had been designed for much greater speed specifically so that she could outrun them. When she fell to sabotage it was a colossal blow to the Allied war effort, and in response a naval intelligence officer, Anthony Marsloe, decid-

Lucky Luciano

ed to enlist the help of the New York Mafia because he knew they were in control of all commercial activity on the docks.

The subterfuge by foreign intelligence agents ceased, but the price America paid was calamitous. Because getting the Mafia's help meant getting permission from the "Boss of Bosses," Lucky Luciano.

It is one of history's great ironies that the United States government went crawling to the Mafia for help at a moment when the mob themselves had just been severely weakened, and could have been crushed altogether by an administration with enough political will.

The notorious Luciano had just started a 40-year prison sentence in Great Meadow penitentiary, and most of his Sicilian gangsters back home were already behind bars, having been caught up in Mussolini's Mafia purge.

Being himself Italian Mussolini knew there was only one way to deal with the Mafia, and when he came to power he ordered his 'Iron Prefect' Cesare Mori to simply lock up all the Mafia families in Sicily; which wasn't exactly difficult because everybody knew who they were.

Of course after the Allied invasion of Sicily Marsloe then compounded his error by choosing Sicilian Americans like New York mayor Charles Poletti, and OSS officer Joseph Russo, whose father was born in Corleone, to head AMGOT: the allied military government, whose job it was to restore community cohesion on the island.

And of course their way of doing this was not only to let all the Mafiosi out of jail, they even made known mob bosses like Genco Russo, and Don Calogero Vizini, into the heads of local government and gave them full civilian and military power over the island.

So this was the accident of history through which the Mafia began its relationship with American military intelligence.

It was a catastrophe for Italy, which has been ruled over by organized crime ever since: it was a catastrophe for Sicily, which suffered a brutal murder every three days in the post-war period: and it was a catastrophe for America, which saw many once-vibrant communities, particularly in New Jersey, have the heart ripped out of them by Mafia extortion and drug-dealing.

Lucky Luciano was deported, after being released from jail, and having found a kindred spirit in another secret organization, the newly-created Central Intelligence Agency, he was then able to combine the activities of organized crime, particularly international drug-running, with smuggling of American-made weapons.

This unholy alliance gave the world its first ever pirates who flew aeroplanes. That is what these people became, pirates with aeroplanes.

The CIA became the world's primary importer-exporter of narcotics, and used the colossal profits to fuel wars around the world thereby enabling their friends in the military industrial complex to sell yet more weapons.

Under the disguise of liberal democracy these men who had financed Hitler, became the enemies of liberty and democracy on a planet-wide basis; and as if to underline their Nazi credentials they also hired all of the former German Nazi intelligence officers, like Reinhard Gehlen, who were out of a job at the end of the war, and brought them into the fold at the beginning of the Cold War, even though they were perfectly well aware that these men had committed genocide, and should have been prosecuted as war criminals.

Reinhard Gehlen

Their attitude quite clearly was that as they had paid for Nazi Germany they were entitled to pick over its carcass in any way they chose.

This was yet another political catastrophe for the United States, because these were the people who put together the notorious "Operation Paperclip," which rounded up all of the Nazi rocket scientists like Werner von Braun, and put them to work for their new American Nazi owners to give them for the first time in human history ICBM's with nuclear warheads.

They became the first men ever to have the power to destroy the whole world at the touch of a button, and it was clear to many observers at the time that it all rather went to their heads.

They saw themselves as giants who were looking down and laughing upon this planet of tiny fools who were stupid enough to go on and on killing each other while they sold arms to both sides throughout the Second World War.

Focke-Wolf aeroplanes which bombed American soldiers were manufactured by AT&T. Allied sailors were drowning in a freezing North Atlantic because their convoys were sunk by guns of Nazi battleships which swivelled on American-made ball-bearings. American soldiers were crushed under the wheels of tanks and trucks made by Henry Ford and John Rockefeller; and gassed to death by the same people.

Sam Giancana took the trouble to explain how this cynical process worked by composing just one, terse, simple sentence which his brother wrote down for posterity.

Extract from the 1964 movie *Dr. Strangelove*

GENERAL JACK RIPPER: I can no longer sit back and allow Communist infiltration, Communist indoctrination, Communist subversion, and the International Communist conspiracy to sap and impurify all of our precious bodily fluids!

"People give their lives" he said "just so a few fat cats can make a killing" and this was precisely what Smedley Butler had tried to explain to the world with his book *War is a Racket*.

At the war's end the rich elite found fortune continuing to smile on them. Firstly they were able to control the utter farce of the Nuremberg trials, which should have hanged every single American merchant banker and leading industrialist.

As it was their contribution to world war two remained hidden from public scrutiny, and they were even allowed to gerrymander light sentences for their German Nazi friends, like Hjalmar Schact, who got off with just a few years and later retired as a billionaire.

But best of all was that the one man who might have been a check to their power passed away as soon as the war was over, and with President Roosevelt gone, and their first Nazi glove puppet Hitler also deceased, it became necessary for Prescott Bush to find another young politician to sponsor.

In true American fashion he decided to advertise: he placed an ad in the *Los Angeles Times* which candidly explained that a group of rich businessmen were seeking a young, ambitious, immoral and most definitely malleable politician who might one day run for President. The ad was deliberately worded in this cynical way because they knew that only an evil, slimy, and completely incorrigible little creep would ever dream of applying for the position.

That was what they wanted. And that was what they got: in the shape of a certain Richard Nixon, here being congratulated on his success by his new master Prescott Bush; and not long after this picture was taken in 1947 Nixon engaged the services of a Jewish gangster who was working for Sam Giancana called Jacob Rubinstein: a man whom the world would one day come to know as Jack Ruby.

Having bought themselves a new political puppet this nefarious band of twentieth-century robber barons now took stock of their situation.

"The Hitler project," as this rich elite called it, could hardly have turned out very much better: their businesses had made colossal profits. Prescott had got his Union Bank back. The Communist menace they so wanted to contain had almost sank back in the Middle Ages with the ravages of war, and best of all was that they had now achieved the very world-domination which Hitler had dreamed about.

They knew that in this new age of modern telecommunications and high-speed jet travel that they had become the first group of robber barons in human history to dominate the entire globe, because they realized there was now absolutely no-one left who could stop them from doing whatever they wanted to do next.

However they also realized that bombed-out and dilapidated Europe would not be able to bear another war for many decades, this was why they now decided that their obscene business profits could only keep coming in if they moved their game of phoney war into the third world – and this was how the CIA came to instigate conflict throughout the Middle East; Southeast Asia and Central America.

Chuck Giancana well remembers a conversation that he had with his Mafia boss brother Sam during this period in which he questioned him with genuine anxiety about the Communist Menace spreading throughout the world.

The TV news was painting a sinister picture of a Soviet enemy with millions of fifth columnists which was intent upon taking over the entire planet. Hadn't he heard of the domino theory? and wasn't he worried about it? In response Sam Giancana simply smiled at his kid brothers' naivety, and he asked him, didn't he realize that the United States (by which he meant the shadow government, not the official one) wanted to take over the world as well? And that the whole idea of communism was just the excuse they were using to do it? He told him that in China they had already succeeded in getting a member of the Chinese mafia, a brutal gangster called Mao Tse Tung, into power just so they could sell more cigarettes in Asia. Communism was just their excuse; and it was pretty much the same story in the Philippines with a crooked politician the Mafia levered into power called Ferdinand Marcos.

Sam "Momo" Giancana

Mao Tse-Tung

Ferdinand Marcos

As for the United States big brother Sam explained that the fat cats were fully aware that Americans will do anything for patriotism, hence you must always provide them with an enemy; a boogeyman.

They won't overwork themselves just to make huge profits for fat cats for any other reason, so new enemies had to be found, or created.

This is what Joe McCarthy's Reds-under-the-bed scare had really been all about: and they used the same excuse in Laos, Chile, Guatemala, El Salvador, Iran. Honduras, Vietnam and Cuba.

If a small country refused to go along with American business interests – which basically meant with the rights of Western multinationals to pay slave wages to third-world peasant farmers growing commodities like tobacco or sugar or fruit, they simply labelled them as Communist, assassinated the democratically-elected head of state with teams recruited from their secret societies the Central Intelligence Agency and the Mafia, and put in a man favourable to their interests, as with the Shah in Iran: simple.

And even more to this Giancana explained to his brother that the political game at home had to be played in the same way as the phoney war game abroad: the lesson was that a businessman always protects his interests by playing both sides.

Sam Giancana knew that the Second World War had been exactly the same as all the CIA's covert wars during the 1950's. They were conducted in order to make more money for the super-rich because in every case they were selling weapons and fuel to both sides, just as they had the Germans.

On the American mainland this cynical attitude manifest itself in the way the gangsters supported the campaign's of both leading candidates in every political head-to-head in order to make sure that whoever got elected he was always their man, and on their side.

So this was the *real* political world which the young senator John F. Kennedy became a part of in 1950's America.

It was a world ruled by a super-rich cabal of secret Nazis who had built the Fascist war machine and concentration camps purely to protect themselves and their money from socialist Russia.

1960 Kennedy/Nixon TV Debate

Having avoided prosecution for the greatest crime in human history they were confident that they could kill anyone and get away with it: particularly if it was someone who might interfere with their power to instigate phoney wars in order to make huge fortunes by lending money and selling weapons to both sides.

The war in which he himself had bravely fought was a sham.

And even John F. Kennedy did not understand this.

Or perhaps we should say that he didn't fully understand what was going on. He and his younger brother Bobby were certainly all too keenly aware of the extent to which their country was in the grip of organized crime, because their own Father, the patriarch Joseph P. Kennedy had made his personal fortune

Joseph P. Kennedy

49

from running illegal liquor during the days of prohibition – activities which earned him the nickname "Bootlegger Joe."

Experienced people are aware that the tendency of each new generation to reject the ideas of the previous generation is an abiding characteristic in human affairs, and it is perfectly plain that with Jack and Bobby it had the effect of making both men highly principled. Their own father had associated with crooks and gangsters, and it was quite clear from their style and their outlook that they had made a commitment to make up for the sins of their father by rejecting this sinister world of hoods and crooks and corrupt politicians by being honest and decent.

If you take a look at any group photo from the early days it's clear these men are being determinedly clean-cut, with the accent heavily on the clean part.

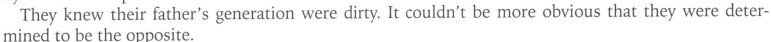

Bobby, Teddy and Jack

They knew their father's generation were dirty. It couldn't be more obvious that they were determined to be the opposite.

The question was how were they going to free themselves? and their country, from the entanglements of the crooked politicians? and the psychopathic Mafia dons? who together were controlling the whole of American life like some multi-legged Fascist Octopus?

How they were going to pull this off was something they were discussing ad nauseam when in the late 1950's they found out their father was in big trouble. A contract had been taken out on Joe Kennedy's life by the Purple Gang; the Jewish mafia of New York, who had accused him of swindling them out of a fortune. Joe Kennedy was really scared, and he turned for help toward the one man in North America who he knew had the power to get the contract called off – Sam Giancana.

Giancana had done business with Kennedy for years, so he agreed to help but, he wanted something for it. He was all too aware of Joe's political ambitions for his son, and of JFK's outstanding good looks.

He wanted assurances that if Jack one day made it to the White House Joe Kennedy would see to it that the heat the two brothers had been trying to turn up on the Mafia would be turned down, and according to Chuck and Sam Giancana junior, Joseph P. Kennedy, just to save his own skin, agreed.

In this way a very confused situation was created, because Sam Giancana, the very kind of mob boss whom the Kennedys had been fighting so hard, through the McClellan committee, to put in jail now thought that they should, and would be, grateful to him.

It was this expectation, and this misunderstanding, which now led Giancana to try to draw the Kennedy's more and more into his dark world – something which he appeared to be succeeding with in the way that first Peter Lawford, and then Frank Sinatra, established relationships with both men.

Extract from Bobby Kennedy's interrogation of Sam Giancana before the McClellan Committee

KENNEDY: Can you tell us anything about any of your operations or are you just going to giggle every time I ask you a question?
GIANCANA: I decline to answer because I believe my answer might tend to incriminate me.
KENNEDY: I thought only little girls giggled Mr. Giancana?

Lawford married Kennedy's sister. Sinatra was putting together campaigning jingles, and it must have seemed to many insiders at the time that when Sam Giancana went around boasting that, as usual, he had everything under control, and that when Jack got to the White House it was going to be a dream ticket for the Mafia; that it must all be true.

Frank and Jack

Judith C. Exner

His boys appeared to be partying together and those who were in the know were aware that JFK had at least some sort of relationship with Judith Campbell Exner, Sam Giancana's girlfriend.

What we haven't known until now is that JFK was hoodwinking Giancana all along.

The role that Judy Campbell played was mostly that of a go-between. What Kennedy was doing through her was giving Giancana FBI reports on mob bosses to make him think that law enforcement were not all that well-informed about the Mafia's scams and their movements, nor even terribly interested.

What Giancana did not know was that the FBI reports he was receiving were carefully selected and most definitely incomplete. Kennedy was not helping Giancana. He was not keeping him in the picture: what he was doing was pulling the wool over his eyes.

For the first time in his life Sam Giancana was perplexed; and he became even more confused when there was a sudden freezing over of relations.

JFK abruptly ended his relationship with Sinatra, and Judy Campbell suddenly found the White House were refusing her calls.

Even more to this Giancana's limitations were shown up in the way he completely failed to comprehend that Kennedy truly was decent and honest. He apparently had many conversations with Murray "the Camel" Humphreys around this time in which both were reassuring each other that Kennedy's White-Knight lifestyle was just a political game to make him look good.

Quite clearly this cynical outlook was the product of living in their dark and corrupt world. They had never known an honest and decent man because in the Mafia there's no such thing.

There is no record of what was said during the three meetings which JFK had with Giancana and his father at the Fontainebleau Hotel just prior to the 1960 general election; but it does now seem that in this most titanic battle of wits between the craftiest criminal in America and the most brilliant politician the world had ever seen Kennedy had won.

JFK Inauguration

He had played the Mafia at their own game. and played it better. Why did John F. Kennedy do this? because he must haveknown just what a dangerous game he was playing. There certainly appears to be no doubt, now that we ourselves are aware of the all-pervading influence of organized crime in America at that time, that this brave and decent, and honest man had realized that he could never get rid of the Mafia and their deadly Fascist friends in politics, industry and banking without first enlisting their help. He had to trick them.

And with this new understanding we can now see, for the first time, with the correct perspective, the motives, characters, intrigues and diverse political interests which were gathering against President Kennedy when he took the oath of office.

Organized crime were fearful of JFK before he ascended to power because the shrewdest amongst them were getting a sense that he had out-foxed and out-manoeuvred the all-powerful Mafia bosses.

But the big mistake researchers have made in the past has been to not understand that every American Oligarch; the big oilmen, the captains of industry; the merchant bankers; the intelligence chiefs; were all crooks and gangsters as well!

The biggest crook in the land was the head of law enforcement J Edgar Hoover. This is what historians have failed to understand until now.

When JFK appointed his 32 year-old kid brother to the post of Attorney General these people collectively froze.

It now fully hit home that JFK really was honest and decent. It hit home that he wanted to make his country as honest and decent as he was, and that he actually believed that with the help of his energetic and determined crime-busting brother that he could do it.

His attitude of course stood in marked contrast to the man whom Kennedy was saddled with as his running mate.

Anyone who has any doubts about the moral rectitude of the average American politician of that time has only to look at the career of Lyndon Baines Johnson to see that generally speaking they were worse than the Mafia itself.

From his involvement with the box 13 scandal and through all of his dealings with his crooked Texan business associate Billy Sol Estes, LBJ proved again and again that he was every bit as unscrupulous as any mob boss, and willing to do absolutely anything for power.

This was a man who'd had his own sister Josefa murdered by his personal hitman, a highly intelligent and psychopathic killer named Malcolm Wallace, who later shot dead the golf professional John Douglas Kinser.

When this case came to court it revealed to the American public how totally corrupt the justice system had become, because LBJ was able to get Wallace off with a five-year suspended sentence. Found guilty of "murder one" he walked free that very day.

This was the sort of corruption which was running rife through the American political system when Fidel Castro overthrew the right-wing government of Fulgencio Batista in 1959

Fidel Castro

Few people are aware that by this advanced stage in their relationship the CIA and the Mafia were together employing the Giancana tactic of supporting both sides in a war.

For many years beforehand they had been supporting Fidel Castro, and not just the Batista regime as many think, by smuggling in both arms and mercenaries to aid the peasant farmers.

One of these mercenaries, an Italian-American called Frank Fiorini, later came to play a pivotal role both in the assassination and subsequent cover-up under his assumed name Frank Sturgis.

Fulgencio Batista

Sturgis and Castro were photographed together many times during the Cuban Revolution, but after Castro enlisted the help of the Russian Soviets Sturgis turned against him.

Like many in the CIA/Mafia Network he felt double-crossed when Castro closed the island's casinos and nationalized all Cuban business. He therefore joined forces with men like Bernard Barker, a member of Batista's secret police, and other Cuban ex-pats who had fled en-masse to Miami Florida, and who now sat together on the American mainland as a very disgruntled and highly politicized splinter group.

Of course to the American Nazis who had bankrolled Hitler this was intolerable: it was a commercial disaster.

Frank Fiorini/Sturgis

Coca-Cola had made millions in easy profits using dirt cheap Cuban sugar grown by dirt-poor Cuban peasants: they were now being told by an upstart third-world dictator that they would have to pay for sugar at the normal market rate. And the mafia were losing millions every single day from the loss of illegal gambling. America's Nazi shadow government therefore decided that someone was going to have to mould this loosely-knit group of disgruntled anti-Castro Cubans into a crack invasion force to retake the island.

Having put their heads together Dulles and Harriman and Richard Bissell decided this would be an excellent job for Prescott's eldest son, George Herbert Walker Bush. A chance for him to prove himself, along with one of his Texas oil business associates: Jack Alston Crichton.

Together these two recruited and trained the Cubans for several terrorist groups known as Operation 40; Alpha 66; ZR/Rifle and Operation Mongoose.

Renegade bands of merciless assassins, who would kill Castro, and who could later be counted on to eliminate any other third world leaders who dared to interfere with American commercial interests.

It was this diverse and unsavoury stream of political intrigue which produced President Kennedy's first great political crisis: the Bay of Pigs in 1962.

Left to right: Allen Dulles, Richard Bissell, President Kennedy, John McCone. April 1962

Jack Alston Crichton

By this time JFK was well aware that the CIA was something much more like a private firm, or a family.

He wasn't surprised when they invaded Cuba without his permission because he knew they were totally out of control. His antipathy led him to cancel the promised air support, and inevitably the invasion failed. The anti-Castro Cubans were mostly captured, and Kennedy then tried to add insult to injury by ordering J Edgar Hoover's FBI to close down the camps where the Cubans were trained.

He even allowed Nikita Khrushchev, the Soviet leader, to inspect the anti-Castro Cuban camps to see they were closed so this could never happen again.

Having only just escaped with his life at the Bay of Pigs it was pretty clear that Frank Sturgis was more than a little annoyed.

This then is how the stage was set for the Kennedy assassination; and when one remembers the colossal number of ruthless and hideously brutal men who had created this situation it's perhaps a little ironic that a peripheral figure in the cast of characters who actually put the plot together was an attractive young woman.

Nineteen year-old Marita Lorenz love affair with Fidel Castro, and her subsequent recruitment as a CIA assassin by Frank Sturgis to kill him, is a very well-known story because it was made into a Feature Film. In spite of her failure to kill the Cuban leader Lorenz continued to associate with the assassination squads trained by the CIA, and it was largely her testimony in the *Spotlight Magazine* trial, after a skilfull cross-examination by Mark Lane, which gave us a window through which we can now see who really participated in the Kennedy assassination, and who was really behind it all.

Extract from an interview with an aggressive Frank Sturgis

"He was scared because Khrushchev says don't do this or we're gonna do that, you know? so he didn't do it; and he deserted the Bay of Pigs. I was involved in the Bay of Pigs, you got a lot of people who were friends of mine that were killed in the Bay of Pigs; and I resent that! Don't play political games with me, I'm a military man, I'm a soldier. I go fight: but damn it if I risk my ass out there, and I'm getting shot at, I don't want some stupid-ass politician to go ahead and make deals behind my back where my people or maybe myself are going to get killed. I don't like that! (threatening tone)

Marita and Fidel

First of all, after the Bay of Pigs invasion, Kennedy had fired Allen Dulles, Richard Bissell and General Charles Cabell for essentially using the CIA as their personal hit men after he found out that Robert Maheu had sought Sam Giancana's permission to talk to his underboss John Roselli about the possibility of a hit on Fidel Castro.

Here you have a government agency, funded by the American taxpayer, associating with the very organized crime racketeers JFK was trying to put in jail for the purpose of carrying out political murders. The President was incensed. Historians have never been surprised that he vowed to smash the CIA into a thousand pieces. It hardly takes a genius to see why the CIA wanted to kill him.

What is more Jack Alston Crichton, and the lifelong friends of Allen Dulles, the Bush family, had just recently purchased exclusive access to 15 million acres of Cuba: almost half the entire island, in order to drill for oil. When he came to power Castro reduced this to a mere twenty thousand acres; a colossal investment which now failed and which led to Crichton's C.V.O.V.T. oil exploration company being de-listed from the stock exchange at a loss of 30 million dollars.

Crichton and George Bush's friends the Texas oil billionaires Clint Murchison and Haroldson Lafayette Hunt also knew that Kennedy wanted to end their most vital tax break – the oil depletion allowance, and their bosom buddy Vice-President Lyndon Johnson was standing at this time with one foot in jail and the other on a banana skin due to his involvement in the corruption scandal now breaking around his favourite assistant Bobby Baker.

LBJ knew his life was finished if Kennedy lived, and he would become President himself if Kennedy died; so his involvement in the plot is hardly difficult to understand, and even more to this the heads both of the U.S. military and the military industrial complex which supplied them (exactly the same Nazis who had supported Hitler in World War II) were fully aware that Kennedy wanted to pull out of Vietnam in a move which would have eventually cost them billions in lost weapons sales.

This circle of thugs and pirates was completed by LBJ's next-door neighbour J Edgar Hoover, who had himself invested millions in Clint Murchison's oil business; just like his Mafia associate Vito Genovese.

Stepping back to look upon this rogues gallery it really is remarkable how Kennedy had managed to make an enemy out of every single dirty hood, every corrupt politician, and every single Nazi businessman living in the country at that time.

It is highly misleading even to see these groups as separate, because the truth is that they were all brutal Fascists who saw nothing wrong in killing to get their own way. The question now was: how were they going to get him? Because we must never forget that generals, admirals, Mafia dons, intelligence chiefs, corrupt politicians and oil billionaires are only people. None of them wanted to go to the electric chair for conspiracy to murder

Clint Murchison

H.L. Hunt

Bobby Baker & LBJ

Vito Genovese

the President. They knew that they had to put together a plan which could not fail to both kill Kennedy, and then cover-up afterwards the fact that they did it.

They knew that in men like Frank Sturgis, his Cuban assassination squads, and the mafia hit-men working with the CIA they had a huge pool of killers to choose from who were ready, able and willing to do the deed. All the same, how could they possibly get to Kennedy? Because they knew that at least in Washington all American Presidents are extremely well protected by the Secret Service.

The most important first step was to engage the age-old Mafia tactic of finding a patsy.

To this end they turned to George de Mohrenschildt: a very sophisticated exiled Russian Count and CIA agent who was close friends in the oil business with George Bush and the Texas oilmen.

George de Mohrenschildt

They were aware that they needed someone like Guiseppe Zangara who appeared to be a low-life discontented misfit, so they chose a low-level CIA operative who had been groomed precisely in order to appear to be a low-life discontented misfit: enter Lee Harvey Oswald; who was carefully handled by de Mohrenschildt as he was placed like a chess-piece in the Texas School Book Depository.

With the patsy selected the combined heads of the American Nazis now sat down together to discuss their problem.

Q1. How do you kill a man riding in an open car on a public street in front of hordes of people without being seen?

Q2. And then how do you cover up forever afterwards the fact that this was a conspiracy? and not the work of a 'lone nut'?

The plotters were keenly aware that it was the second question which posed the biggest problem.

The professional military men, like Colonel Edward Lansdale and Admiral George Burkley, Kennedy's personal physician were well aware that there are any number of ways to hide or disguise a sniper: behind trees; inside other vehicles; behind windows in office buildings; but this was a plot which had to have an absolute guarantee of success.

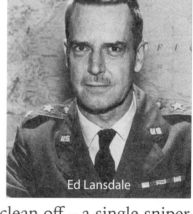
Ed Lansdale

If a squad of riflemen were all to fire at their target at the same time this would certainly guarantee the man's death, but the subsequent police investigation would instantly realize more than one shooter was involved.

A team of gunmen all firing together might actually blow Kennedy's head clean off – a single sniper couldn't do that: so what were they to do?

It was during these deliberations that a macabre thought first registered.

They would have to control the body after the shooting. In order to make sure that all physical evidence available to police forensic scientists conformed to the scenario of a single assassin.

And just how in the hell were they going to do that?

By way of preparing the ground Sam Giancana now ordered Richard Nixon's political associate Jack Ruby to keep Oswald snug under his wing, and then to set about hiring the best local riflemen; preferred candidates being men like his close friend Charles Voyd Harrelson: the father of Hollywood

Charles Voyd Harrelson

actor Woody Harrelson, who had proven his hit-man credentials by shooting dead dozens of men for money.

He then turned to his Mafia associates Carlos Marcello and Santos Trafficante to supply the best gunman from their cities, while he himself instructed the well-known underboss Tony Accardo to give the Chicago end of the contract to Giancana's favourite and most trusted hoodlums, Charles Nicoletti and Milwaukee Phil Alderisio.

Carlos Marcello

This pair had to be flown in 1500 miles to the ranch of Mafia Hood Peter Licavoli, and then driven the remaining six hundred miles to Dallas. It had been agreed with Giancana's and Genovese's oil business partners H.L. Hunt and Clint Murchison, that every gunman would be paid fifty thousand dollars for the hit, and that the oil men would stump up the cash so there was no way of tracing it back to either the mob or the CIA.

For their apart Jack Crichton and George Bush were trying to lay the groundwork at the street level with the mayor Earle Cabell, the brother of CIA Deputy Director Charles Cabell, whom Kennedy had fired.

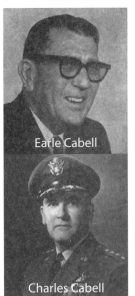
Earle Cabell

Charles Cabell

Both the Cabell brothers were crucially important in the development of the fine details of the plot, because they agreed to allow Crichton and his associates George Lumpkin, the Dallas Deputy Police Chief, Lieutenant Colonel George Whitmeyer and Harry Weatherford to make use of their 488th military intelligence detachment; a privately funded part-time Intelligence Force which had amongst its ranks many members of the John Birch Society, the Ku Klux Klan, and around half of all the serving police officers in Dallas.

Santos Trafficante

Tony Accardo

The plotters realized this was a masterstroke, because it meant they could control the streets and the crime scene, but they also realized that when the shooting occurred the response of at least half the police on duty would appear to be completely genuine.

And yet for all this intricate planning, involving as Sam Giancana later admitted, dozens of men, the American Nazis were aware they still had a problem.

Getting the snipers into position and coordinating their fire by radio was not too difficult – it's something the military do every day; but this problem of blowing the man's head clean off had another side to it. Supposing, as can happen, all the snipers missed? How could they possibly legislate for this contingency?

You see being a professional sniper is a lot like being a professional golfer: everyone knows that generally speaking a golf pro on a par 3 will hit the green: but even the world's best occasionally miss by a wide margin and the same can happen to any rifleman.

We can be quite certain that the guiding brains of the American Nazis; Allen Dulles and David Attlee Phillips, in order to cover this eventuality, must have at least considered having one assassin run up to the limousine to attempt a point-blank range Mafia-style shooting should the others miss – but then another problem appeared.

Supposing their assassin couldn't run quick enough to jump on a speeding car?

Little by little the realisation hit home. The plot could even wind up looking silly, and themselves ridiculous. There was only one answer. They would have to control the President's protection: the Secret Service.

Extract from an interview with Gerry P. Hemming

INTERVIEWER: Were you ever offered money to assassinate President Kennedy?
HEMMING: Directly. On numerous occasions.

Marita Lorenz testified, under oath, that in late November of 1963 she drove from Miami to Dallas Texas with Frank Sturgis, followed by a back-up car which contained a stash of weapons. Travelling along with them were Gerry Patrick Hemming, an American mercenary like Sturgis … two Cuban brothers, Ignacio and Guillermo Novo-Sampol, a Cuban pilot called Pedro Diaz Lanz, and his friend Orlando Bosch.

At first Marita assumed this was to be just another arms-smuggling engagement just like many others she'd been on with Sturgis before.

Orlando Bosch

However, when they reached their Dallas motel they were visited by someone Marita had met many times before: CIA agent E. Howard Hunt who stayed almost an hour, and paid Sturgis with cash stuffed in a very large envelope.

E. Howard Hunt

This was the evening of November 21st 1963, and Marita began to get worried. She knew that President Kennedy was visiting Dallas the next day. Becoming concerned she pressed Sturgis as to the real purpose of the visit? and when he told her that for this one time it had to be confidential she decided she wanted out.

Marita had no way of knowing that a great number of other people had made similar journeys that day. CIA pilot Tosh Plumlee flew several assassins into Dallas Love Field without even being told who they were.

From all over the country radio operators, rifle men, drivers, false ID suppliers like Chauncey Holt and Bernard Barker, and getaway pilots like David Ferrie converged on the city: whilst at the home of oilman Clint Murchison a group of his Nazi friends were congregating to celebrate Kennedy's imminent demise.

Due to the testimony of LBJ's mistress Madelaine Duncan Brown the mother of his illegitimate son, we now know that amongst these guests were: J. Edgar Hoover, and his homosexual lover Clyde Tolson, who stood to lose the millions they'd invested in their hosts oil business if Kennedy lived – Hoover also knew Kennedy wanted to replace him as head of the FBI. The two Brown brothers of Brown & Root who, along with Cliff Carter, John Connally and Senator Ralph Yarborough, stood to lose millions from lost defence contracts because they knew JFK wanted to end the Vietnam War. Also present were Joseph Sevilla, head of the Mafia in Dallas, and the mayor of Dallas Earle Cabell, the CIA men who knew the President was serious about smashing the Central Intelligence Agency because he'd already fired Cabell's brother Charles.

David Ferrie

Madelaine Duncan Brown

John McCloy

Having a drink with them was Chase Manhattan Bank chief John McCloy a confirmed Nazi who had shared a box with Hitler at the 1936 Berlin Olympic Games, and Mafia chieftain Carlos Marcello, who felt nicely at home rubbing shoulders with Sam Giancana's representatives Jack Ruby, Richard Nixon and Haroldson Lafayette Hunt. The media were represented by a Amon G. Carter, and the only one who might have felt a little out of place as he awaited his boss was the world-class marksman and serial killer Malcolm Wallace.

Johnson strode over to her and said fiercely …

AFTER TOMORROW THOSE GODDAMN KENNEDYS WILL NEVER EMBARRASS ME AGAIN—

--THAT'S NO THREAT, THAT'S A PROMISE!

Late in the evening Lyndon Baines Johnson finally turned up and briefly went into the party.

When he came out to greet Madelaine Brown she said he was euphoric:

Johnson had clearly been told by the people in that room that everything was ready.

The next morning the President landed at Love Field and was led to his car by Governor John Connally. As he is driven away it is immediately apparent that something is wrong as Secret Service agent Henry J. Rybka tries to take up his proper position on the President's limousine, holding on to handles provided for the purpose, and is ordered to stand down by Emory Roberts.

Let's just look at Rybka's reaction again. He is quite clearly disgusted. Why aren't they letting him do his job? and as the car glides into Dallas we can now see how the removal of his Secret Service protection has opened the President up to a field of fire from almost any direction. It's plain from these pictures that as the motorcade moved on into Dallas the Secret Service meant to protect the President remained crowded together on the vehicle behind – while travelling in the pilot car some 400 yards ahead three men are smiling as they see everything is going to plan.

Extract from Madelaine D. Brown interview by Robert Gaylon Ross

Ross: Let's go back to the night before, when Johnson came out of the meeting, what did he say to you?

Brown: He was so angry. He a violent temper when he was upset.

Ross: Well let's use the exact words that he said to you? what did he say to you?

Brown: He grabbed me by the arm, and he had this deep voice, and he said: "after tomorrow and those S.O.B.'s will never embarrass me again! That's no threat … that's a promise!"

Crichton, Lumpkin and Whitmeyer have used their influence to remove the military protection which should have been amongst the crowd; and whilst the people lining the parade route are ten deep in places Lumpkin has seen to it the police have let almost no one into the would-be crime scene.

Pausing at the corner of Houston and Elm Lumpkin is seen exchanging reassurances with one of his men. Yes, he tells him. The hit is on. Glancing discreetly upwards he sees Weatherford and the best Cuban sniper, Eladio del Valle preparing to fire. The signal is passed to the other snipers to get into position.

Having been let into the Dal-Tex building by oil baron Haroldson Hunt, Eugene Hale Brading unlocks the second floor broom closet.

Eladio del Valle

Eugene Hale Brading

A client of New Orleans lawyer G. Wray Gill, who also represents Mafia boss Carlos Marcello, Brading has a getaway pilot waiting whom Gill employs as a Private Detective: David Ferrie.

He opens the window, and as Charles Nicoletti loads his rifle Richard Cain listens to his radio. Car coming. Get ready.

Closing the door Milwaukee Phil Alderisio guards the corridor with two Cubans; Rolando Masferrer and Rolando Otero.

This basic pattern was established all over the plaza. A sniper, next to a radioman, alongside a second marksman who could take over should the first want to back out at the last moment.

Each team was then guarded by more assassins, mainly Cubans, who made sure no-one interfered with each group. It all sounds quite professional and the truth is, it was.

Sam Giancana's spy in the Chicago police force, Richard Cain, was an electronics and wiretapping expert who spoke five languages.

Up on the grassy knoll with his childhood friend Charles Harrelson stood the diminutive Charles Frederick Rogers; a nuclear physicist who worked in seismology for Shell oil, he was also friends with David Ferrie in the Civil Air Patrol.

Up in the Texas School Book Depository LBJ's psychotic hitman Malcolm Wallace held a PhD and taught at the University of Texas. The Texas oilmen, Mafia dons, merchant bankers and military industrialists had assembled the all-time dream-team of professional killers.

They were there to make absolutely certain their King died. And the two men who in later years would steal his crown, Richard Millhouse Nixon and George Herbert Walker Bush, smiled from the sidewalk as they exchanged winks with Jack Crichton. There was no way Kennedy could escape now and they knew it.

Arranging his sniper's nest at the other end of the sixth floor Sturgis was the first to be spotted, by Arnold Rowland.

A moment later fifteen-year-old Amos Euins caught sight of one of the Sturgis-trained Cubans, Ignacio Novo-Sampol. Even more significantly Richard Randolph Carr, a steel construction-worker who was looking for a job in the new Dallas courthouse, which was then under construction, stared out from his seventh floor vantage point and saw Malcolm Wallace taking position to fire.

Charles F. Rogers   Malcolm Wallace

Extract from TV interview with Arnold Rowland

ROWLAND: I just looking around when we noticed this man up in the window, and I remarked to my wife – tried to point him out – and remarked that he must be a security guard, Secret Service agent.

INTERVIEWER: So the window then that you're referring to is on the opposite end of the building from where the main entrance to the building is?

ROWLAND: Yes, it is on the other side of the building, (pointing to the opposite end of the school book depository away from the "Oswald" window) and he had a rifle. It looked like a high-powered rifle because it had a scope which looked in relation to the size of the rifle to be a big scope.

Testifying at the trial of Clay Shaw he gave a minutely detailed description of a very heavyset man in a sports jacket who wore large-framed glasses. He could see the man so clearly he even said his eyeglasses had large ear-pieces.

Carr

America, the home of the brave and the land of the free, was about to discover that it wasn't what it thought it was. As the President's car made the turn on to Houston government agents who had sworn an oath to uphold their country's democratic principles waited alongside Mafia killers to murder their own commander-in-chief.

One of the men they were working for, Sam Giancana, said this proved that in reality there was no such thing as white hats and black hats. That notion, he said, was just "a sham for saps to cling to."

It was now that Abraham Zapruder pressed the trigger on his 8 millimetre cine-camera. Ever since that moment the world has accepted that what he recorded was the definitive account of what really happened. What people must appreciate is that what they have just seen is not at all what really happened.

So just exactly what did happen during the 10 seconds Zapruder was filming?

TV interview with Judith Campbell Exner

EXNER: One thing I recognized was there are no black hats and there are no white hats; they all conduct themselves the exact same. And very good evidence of that is that the CIA would hire two so-called Mafia men, Sam Giancana and John Roselli to assassinate Fidel Castro. If there's such a difference you're not supposed to have anything to do with each other, but in essence the remark is really they're all in bed together. They all do business together.

To begin with Dulles, Lansdale and David Attlee Phillips had tried to get over the problem of volley-fire blowing the President's head clean off by firing in four stages.

Stage one was meant to be a single shot by Charles Nicoletti into the back of Kennedy's head from the Dal-Tex building some 40-yards behind. Had he succeeded the plotters would have had the single-assassin-with-one-bullet story they wanted; but in his excitement the Mafia assassin squeezed the trigger too soon. His bullet ricocheted off the hard chrome sill of the limo's backseat and struck the curb beneath the overpass, sending up a sharp piece of concrete which scratched James Tague's face.

Watching the Zapruder clip again. We clearly see how this little girl stops running, and her gaze looks directly at where the shot originated, and not up at the sixth floor of the depository.

It was now that umbrella man took over. Standing right at the kerbside it was his job, should the first shot miss, to give a clear visual signal: target is not injured. The intelligence chiefs knew that if this situation occurred Kennedy would now be moving rapidly away from the first sniper. They knew the only way to make sure of getting him was to fusillade the car, so a moment later two rifles tried to fire, from directly in front, at exactly the same time, to deceive witnesses into thinking there was only one shot.

Harrelson's bullet hit JFK in the throat, and another gunman hiding in a culvert 50 yards away

TV interview/confession with Charles Voyd Harrelson

TV INTERVIEWER: You said you'd killed President Kennedy?
HARRELSON: At the same time I said I had killed the Judge I said I had killed Kennedy... well, do you believe Lee Harvey Oswald killed President Kennedy? We'll get back to that. Alone? Without any aid from a rogue agency of the U.S government? or at least a portion of that agency? I believe you're very naive if you do.

Extract from TV interview with Doctor Evalea Glanges

DR. GLANGES: The Presidential limousine was there; I had been staying there for some time just watching the back of the emergency room; talked to my friend next to me and said look, there's a bullet hole in the windshield and pointed it out to them. But it was very clear it was a through-and-through bullet hole, through the windshield of the car, from the front to the back.

up in the embankment of the overpass made the hole in the windscreen which was later seen by Dr Evalea Glanges.

As Kennedy emerges from behind the road sign his distress is clear, while Governor Connally remains composed. This single frame of the Zapruder film makes nonsense of the single Bullet theory because it's quite clear both men have not been struck at the same time.

Kennedy has now passed through two layers of fire and has not been hit in the head. To cover this eventuality the assassins were given a simple instruction – fusillade the car with everything. So that in the next few moments the five remaining riflemen fired, causing the Secret Service agent riding in the front passenger seat, Roy Kellerman, to report a feeling like "a jet sonic boom" as the hail of bullets whistled into the car.

It is now, more than three seconds after Kennedy is hit in the throat, that Frank Sturgis misses his target altogether and blows out five inches of Governor Connolly's ribs; compressing his lungs and puffing his cheeks with a bullet which quite clearly struck at far too steep an angle to come from the other end of the depository.

In almost the same instant Eladio del Valle hit the governor in the wrist; Weatherford fired into his thigh, and Nicoletti's second shot hit the chrome frame of the window.

A moment later the best marksman, Malcom Wallace, shot Kennedy in his upper back, the bullet strike witnessed and recorded by all the Secret Service men in the following car.

Jackie Kennedy starts looking concerned, and yet even now there are no obvious signs that her husband, held upright by his back-brace, has been shot twice.

The assassins have so far failed to hit him in the head, and it is now that they play the ace up their sleeve.

Here we can finally answer the riddle of where, on an empty street, you can hide a man with a rifle, and how he can manage to shoot a man speeding past him in a limousine? The answer is that he can't.

And that is why the driver, William Greer, looked around twice to see whether Kennedy had been hit in the head, and when he saw he hadn't, as dozens of witnesses including police officers confirmed, he stopped the car completely.

It is now that most people have been led to believe that Kennedy was shot in the head by Charles Voyd Harrelson; the sniper standing on the grassy knoll.

This is not true.

Because if we look at the angle of elevation of a shot from that area it's obvious that a shot originating from above and right would have pushed Kennedy's head down and left, whereas it's quite clear that his head is knocked upwards and to the left by the impact.

So where did that bullet come from?

Incredibly the answer has lain hidden in the most well known and iconic image from the assassination of the motorcycle policeman heaving his bike onto its Stand.

Look now as we freeze frame him … here. This is the moment when the whole world was looking up the hill toward the man who had fired from the grassy knoll but that is not where the police officer is looking.

He is looking down.

Into the storm drain.

Because THAT is where that shot, at a stationary car, came from.

The shot which all of the well-known assassination witnesses described as coming from behind the picket fence missed completely, and ripped-up the grass at Jean Hill's feet. She did not even notice, but we know this is true because the FBI told her so.

Extract from TV interview with Presidential motorcade motorcycle cop Bobby Hargis

HARGIS: His orders was to slow down with the rest of the guys.
INTERVIEWER: This is Greer? the driver of the Presidential Limousine?
HARGIS: Yeah, the Presidential Limousine slowed down almost to a stop.

So who were the men who fired unseen from the storm drains on Elm Street? One thing we know is that they were very young, and had to be brought into the conspiracy because they had to crawl into a filthy, smelly sewer. Something which the older, experienced Mafia assassins would never have dreamed of doing. They were basically two kids, looking for excitement.

The first was Curtis Laverne Crafard; also known as Larry Crafard. Formerly CIA he had worked for Jack Ruby at the Carousel Club, and Ruby had told everyone his name was Lee Harvey Oswald – until Lee Harvey Oswald walked in!

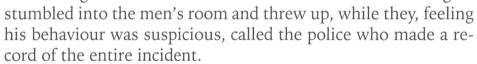

But while above-ground the world was taking pictures, and running, and screaming, and trying to figure out what had happened, the other young man was stumbling along 400 yards of a reeking, fetid Dallas sewer pipe to emerge from this culvert.

And he was not Lee Harvey Oswald, or Roscoe White, or J.D. Tippit, nor even a Cuban or Russian Communist.

His name was Jack Allen Lawrence.

And we know that after stumbling up this bank he turned up 15 minutes later at the Lincoln-Mercury car showroom where he'd obtained a job with false references.

Pale, sweating, and, on a hot sunny day in Dallas, covered in mud.

Telling his co-workers Albert Bogart and Robert Tater he had been ill that morning he stumbled into the men's room and threw up, while they, feeling his behaviour was suspicious, called the police who made a record of the entire incident.

Back at the Plaza the guilt of the radiomen coordinating the gunfire can be seen from their behaviour. These two, Orlando Bosch and the Umbrella Man have a seat while everyone else runs around them. Bosch makes a report that the hit was successful, then casually walks away, just like the chief radio coordinator Jim Hicks, with the radios clearly visible in their back pockets.

A few yards away the CIA's clean-up squad have begun working to remove all evidence useful to a forensic team. Deputy Sheriff Buddy Walthers is here seen finding the bullet which struck in the grass near the manhole cover. He hands it on to one of the fake FBI men, who pockets it.

Lee Bowers

Walthers

While this is going on Rodgers, Harrelson and E. Howard Hunt are discovered hiding in the box cars of the train which they hoped would be their getaway vehicle: until it's prevented from moving by railway dispatcher and key witness Lee Bowers.

They are photographed repeatedly as they are marched to the Dallas courthouse and one can clearly see in this picture the radio receiver Hunt is wearing in his right ear, which is identical to the receivers worn by those Dallas police officers who were part of the plot.

As they walk they are overseen by Colonel Ed Lansdale, who secures their release, and begins to give the press the cover-story that this man (Oswald) is the major suspect and that acting alone he shot the President from behind.

The truth, as we now know, is that eight separate snipers, firing sixteen shots in four separate stages, tried to make certain of killing the President by hitting him in the head and had failed abysmally.

Lansdale

The shooting on the day had been nothing to write home about. A third of all the shots had missed the car completely. Had it not been for the ruse of bribing the driver to brake at a point painted on the kerbside, which is still visible, so that Jack Lawrence could shoot Kennedy in the head from just 15 feet away, the President might have survived.

So now we must address the question – why does the Zapruder film not show this very obvious set up of the Limousine stopping for the head-shot? The answer of course is that it has been tampered with.

In the 1960s Hollywood special-effects teams had developed techniques for masking-off segments of film frames to disguise the true movement of figures within the picture. In the Zapruder film frames have been removed in order to fake a continuous flowing motion so that we don't see the very obvious set-up which dozens of witnesses reported.

If you look now at the top of the frame the doctoring of the film becomes perfectly obvious by the way in which the figures are blurred, and yet the shadows are sharp, which is impossible.

This CIA tampering with the evidence becomes even clearer when the Zapruder film is run next to the Orville Nix film taken from the other side. It's easy to see from the way the motorcycles suddenly close on the Limousine that it stops completely; and we can see that frames have also been removed from the Nix film by the way in which agent Clint Hill appears to move sideways while running forwards before leaping on the car.

As the mad dash to Parkland Hospital begins the chief co-ordinator in the assassination plot, George Herbert Walker Bush, casually relaxes with hands in his pockets at the entrance of the School Book Depository.

Now this is going to be one of those all-too-familiar Kennedy assassination moments in which people will say "well, yes, it could be him, but how can we be sure? because we've seen this kind of thing before with BadgeMan.

However, a gentleman who I think must be a police detective has posted a YouTube video in which he utilizes the latest forensic techniques for identifying murder suspects by making a comparison between the photo taken in Dealey Plaza and one of George Bush in conversation with Richard Nixon during Watergate.

This man points out that this person has exactly the same skull shape,

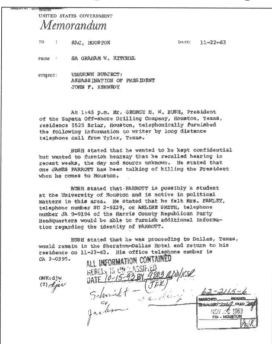

exactly the same hairline, chin and nose as George Bush. He is also wearing the same type of suit, white shirt and exactly the same type of tie. He is exactly the same height, the same weight, is wearing clothing which matches down to his shoes but, most importantly, he has a characteristic mannerism of cocking his right wrist when he puts his hands in his pockets.

We know from this Declassified FBI memo that George Bush was in Dallas, staying at the Sheraton on November 22nd. So can there be any doubt about this person's identity?

Surrounded by the corrupt policeman he was co-ordinating Bush knew already that if an honest officer should happen to catch one of the assassins it would, because of what Mark Lane rightly calls 'plausible deniability' make no difference: because what would they find? Mafia hoods? with prison records as long as their arms? or contract killers like Charles Harrelson?

They certainly wouldn't have found anyone who carried CIA credentials, or anyone whose involvement with the government could be traced.

But even while he smiled and chatted to his fellow killers Bush was unaware that the plotters had just made their first big mistake.

They knew that they had to forensically control the body from the moment the shots were fired, and the moment Kennedy entered Trauma Room One that control had to be relinquished.

Although they had CIA agents placed in the emergency unit these people were not aware of the throat wound, which could hardly be seen because it was so tiny.

It was at this moment that all the Dallas doctors, and Nurses like Aubrey Bell, made a mental note of this very obvious sign of a frontal entry shot.

Extract from TV interview with Dr Crenshaw

DR CRENSHAW: The second wound was here, in the throat, right above the neck-tie; (indicating) It was a small opening, very small, three to five millimeters; about the size of your little finger. I looked at the wound again, I wanted to know, and remember this the rest of my life, and the rest of my life I will always know he was shot from the front.

…and also described the portion missing from the rear of Kennedy's head after the impact of the frangible bullet which hit him in the right temple.

TV INTERVIEWER: The bullet struck about where? and past about where?

DR CRENSHAW: From here (pointing to temple) through, taking out the back of the occipital part: the back of your head, this was gone.

One of the Dallas medical team Dr. Charles Crenshaw, a junior doctor at that time, vividly recalls what the first professionals in the Kennedy killing had to deal with..

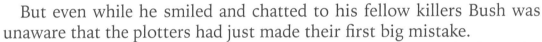

This information soon made it's way to the media, and this is why at the very first press conference press secretary Malcolm Kilduff correctly described the cause of death and direction of the shot.

In order to find a means with which to contradict this evidence the cover-up now began in earnest with the summoning from the Restland funeral home of a CIA agent who was known for being the best in the business at reconstructive surgery on cadavers, John Melvin Liggett.

This man was actually attending a funeral when he was told of the President's assassination and asked to go to Parkland by the coroner. What he did not know as he drove away was that one of his clients in this macabre and gruesome story was at that moment still alive.

John Melvin Liggett

When he was arrested years later by New York police detective Jim Rothstein, Frank Sturgis, on discovering that Rothstein was a Bay of Pigs veteran like himself, got into an old army buddies conversation with him and said first of all that after the assassination he returned to the Miami safe house where he ridiculed Marita Lorenz for missing history. It was all perfectly safe he told her: no cops, no newspaper investigation: everything was covered.

Sturgis then went on to say the Dallas police officer J.D. Tippit was actually gunned down by the radio talk show host G Gordon Liddy who was at that time a CIA agent working with E. Howard Hunt.

Extract from German TV interview with Marita Lorenz

LORENZ: I asked Sturgis "Jesus Christ Frank! did you shoot the President?! Did you have something to do with that??" He said "Bah, who gives a shit? who's gonna prove it?" He said "we kill a lot of people, what the hell's the difference??"

And here we must address a question which puzzled assassination researchers for years: why did a Dallas policeman have to die within a few minutes of President Kennedy? What possible function could he have played in the overall plot as a corpse? one would think the authorities could have caught the fleeing Patsy without any need to incriminate him any further? so why did the life of J.D. Tippit also have to end on the 22nd of November 1963?

Where did he fit in?

In only the last few years a wonderful investigator called Robert D. Morningstar discovered one tiny little fact about Jefferson Davis Tippit which became the most important single piece in the completion of this puzzle.

Because officer Tippit had a nickname. When he was at work his fellow officers always used to call him JFK. Because at 39 years of age he looked exactly like him.

In the only well-known picture of Tippit his Elvis haircut makes him appear very youthful: but having turned grey, and having nearly turned 40, most people felt his resemblance to Kennedy was uncanny.

What Tippit never knew, as he drove past assassination witnesses Jack Tatum, Domingo Benavidez and Aquila Clemens, was that he had been selected to play the role of the President in death.

Researchers have always believed it couldn't be a coincidence that Tippit was shot in the right temple; just like JFK some 45 minutes earlier. They wondered why bullets had been removed from his body in the ambulance? and why, when he was pronounced dead on arrival at the Methodist Hospital, it was felt necessary to move his body to Parkland??

JFK~TIPPIT PHOTOCOMPOSITE
(Copyright 1996, R.D. MORNINGSTAR)

Hill

With their concentration firmly fixed on the casket of the deceased President the newsmen completely ignored the ambulance which spirited away the body of J.D. Tippit so that it could be loaded onto Air Force 2 where John Melvin Liggett was waiting.

When Kennedy's casket arrived at Love Field a few minutes later Clint Hill, the agent who jumped on the car, recalled that all the people aboard Air Force One were told they had to go forward to witness the swearing-in of Lyndon Baines Johnson.

This, of course, was just a ruse to get Jackie Kennedy to leave her husband's body, and the moment she was out of the way his cadaver was stolen, and placed aboard Air Force two next to the cadaver of J.D. Tippit.

Many people have seen this famous picture in which LBJ is smiling at congressman Albert Thomas a moment after becoming President, and he is winking back. We haven't known until now just how huge and terrible a secret he was sharing with Johnson, because at that moment, on the plane right alongside, the most highly qualified specialist in reconstructive surgery and embalming in the country, John Melvin Liggett, was starting to make a facsimile of the dead President using the body of J.D. Tippit in order to obscure the true extent of the damage to Kennedy's head and make it seem consistent with a shot from behind.

But Liggett realized immediately this was well-nigh impossible, because having been told over the radio about the head-shot Liddy took it upon himself to try and ape this damage by firing into Tippit's torso, and then, when he was down, firing into his right temple instead of into the back of the head as he'd been instructed.

This was a second huge mistake.

The human brain has a consistency like play school plasticine. Fire a bullet through it and it is very easy for a skilled pathologist to track the bullet's path at autopsy.

What Liggett wanted to show to any investigators was a brain that looked like this (A).

What he had was one brain which looked like this (B).

And another which looked like this (C).

A large portion of Kennedy's brain had been ripped out by the impact of the explosive or frangible bullet; and what remained was filled with tiny shards of lead, some of them microscopic, which might take all night to locate.

Liggett was terrified. The plotters had asked him to play Doctor Frankenstein at 30,000 feet. Yet with all his embalming experience he instantly realized a botch-job was the best he could possibly deliver.

In his panic he sawed off Tippitt's skull, and simply ripped out the entire brain to at least make sure no-one could track the bullet which, after Liddy's error, had so obviously come from the wrong direction.

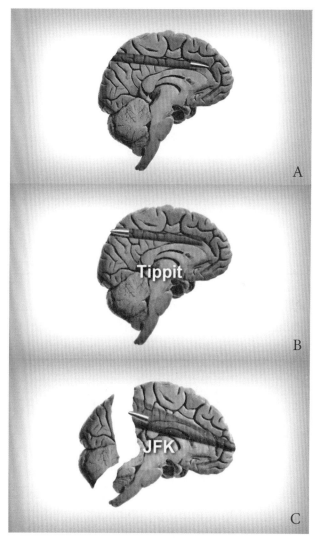

A

Tippit

B

JFK

C

He then compounded Liddy's error by making a large hole in the rear of the head to ape the damage to Kennedy's head. With this done he rebuilt the skull, hurriedly sewed the scalp back together, and then set about the gruesome task of trying to make the cadaver of J.D. Tippit more closely resemble the cadaver of John F Kennedy by shaving eyebrows, bringing forward Tippit's slightly more receding hairline, filling in missing segments of both heads with plaster of paris, and rebuilding portions of the flesh with wax.

Liggett performed this ghoulish service while the aircraft he was on, Air Force Two, went through the usual procedure of leapfrogging Air Force One to arrive at Andrews Air Force Base slightly earlier.

He wasn't given long enough, and in the rush to get finished the plotters now made their third and most stupid mistake.

Instead of placing Tippit's body in a casket identical to the one aboard Air Force One they placed him in a spartan grey metal coffin, inside a body bag.

As the TV media showed these distressing pictures to a world reeling in shock it's hardly surprising that no one ever dreamed this casket could be empty. But it was.

As it was driven away; out of sight of the media, the two bodies were taken from Air Force Two and loaded onto a helicopter. It was at this point that two honest men: FBI agents Francis X. O'Neill and his partner William Siebert, became crucial figures in the story.

They explained to researcher David Lifton that they made the journey to the Naval Hospital at Bethesda in the car behind the hearse which carried Jackie and Bobby and most notably Admiral George Burkley: who made sure he stayed with the empty coffin by sitting on another man's lap.

Upon reaching Bethesda Siebert and O'Neill said Burkley then guided the family members into the building while the hearse was ordered to the rear to unload. But that was where the simplicity ended.

The FBI men and many other witnesses recalled a scene of absolute mayhem in which no one seemed to know what was going on; and military men were rushing around everywhere exchanging anecdotes about decoy ambulances they had been ordered to follow – which had become high-speed chases around the hospital grounds as these vehicles raced away.

It seems this confusion was created with the intention of misleading both the press and the large respectful crowd which had gathered on the lawn. People were asking each other which ambulance contained the President's body? then a rumour started that it was coming by helicopter: but which one? everyone watching that night recalls the air was filled with them.

And the FBI men also told Lifton that in the midst of all this mayhem they helped to carry the casket inside. This was flatly denied by the team of Navy men, who said they did it alone.

It is therefore perfectly clear that *two* bodies were brought to the morgue separately whilst confusion reigned, and it was now that the plotters themselves became confused by the mayhem they had created, because they left J.D.Tippit's cadaver in the wrong casket.

It should have been switched and gone into the autopsy room in the large expensive casket used in Dallas.

Instead mortuary technician Paul O'Connor received a coffin so dull and nondescript no one could believe it had been utilized to transport the body of a President.

The autopsy then became a farce the moment it began.

While Siebert and O'Neill made their now famous and entirely correct observation that the body "seemed to have undergone surgery prior to autopsy – mainly in the head area" Commander Humes himself testified that "the moment he touched the head pieces of the skull fell down onto the autopsy table."

Extract from an interview with Ambulance Driver Aubrey Rike filmed by Lifton himself

RIKE: I helped put President Kennedy's body in a bronze ceremonial casket on November 22nd 1963 at Parkland memorial hospital.

O'CONNOR (4 Hours Later) It was a very plain casket, and when I say plain, I mean it was a pinkish grey: it had pink and grey on the sides. There was nothing fancy about it; as far as being bronze? It wasn't bronze.

That is not possible unless surgery was done before post-mortem. And that surgery could only have been performed aboard the aircraft because there was no other time to do it.

Dr. James Humes then found that he had to try to work with Admirals Burkley, Galloway and Kenny actually touching his elbows, and became increasingly confused and embarrassed himself at his utter failure to find any trace of the bullets which killed the President.

Of course this was hardly surprising considering the President lay dead in an adjoining room; and that Liggett had removed all the bullets from J.D. Tippit.

As the autopsy proceeded O'Connor revealed that Burkley interfered constantly in the procedure, steering Humes away from the torso where he would have found the holes made by Liddy.

And while everyone in the room remained aghast and disturbed by the huge hole in the back of the head, and absence of any brain matter, two porters O'Connor had never seen before came in pushing a trolley which had a sheet on it which hid a small lump.

They had told people in the corridor it was a dead newborn baby, but it turned out be a complete brain, which could only have come from a third cadaver. This was weighed and pickled in formaldehyde before anyone even had a chance to inquire when it had been removed?

The most farcical moment of all came when Humes faced Arlen Specter in front of the Warren Commission, and found the leading council pressing him to say that the wound he found in the back of the head was an entry wound.

His incredible answer was that the bullet could only have entered *and* exited from the rear.

Humes actually told the world that the bullet had done a U-turn inside the President's skull.

Now that we know the truth it may seem remarkable that David Lifton got so close, and yet never quite realized that what he had been investigating for 15 years was a body-switch.

David Lifton

But can we really be surprised? Like so many other decent men Lifton was simply unable to imagine that anyone could ever think up such a grotesque and degenerate conspiracy.

He simply never realized that what he was dealing with was nothing less than the Devil himself: and for those who find all this impossible to accept one of the Devils who murdered JFK, Frank Sturgis, was perfectly candid about how routine body switches had become in the CIA by 1963.

The truth about the autopsy is that the Devils who killed Kennedy messed up very badly. They had wanted to show the world actual photographs of a single bullet wound from behind. As it was they had to resort to a lot of badly faked photographs which critics like Robert Groden easily discredited, and silly drawings which everyone realized did not line up anywhere near the School Book Depository.

With the autopsy over Mrs. Kennedy and the President's brother were shown the body prepared for burial.

Not surprisingly they were wholly unconvinced by Liggett's attempts to make a Dallas police officer look like the President of the United States.

Witnesses there at the time said Bobby scoffed and said "it doesn't look anything like him" while Mrs Kennedy became adamant. "It isn't Jack" she declared "that looks like something you'd find in Madame Tussauds Wax Museum"

Extract from TV interview with Frank Sturgis

Sturgis: There was a switch.
TV Interviewer: A body switch?
Sturgis: A body switch yes. (holding up two fingers)

Many people have studied this alleged picture of the President's remains, and wondered how it could possibly be John F. Kennedy? when the Zapruder film clearly shows this right temple area being blown apart by the impact of the frangible bullet?

The simple answer is that this is not JFK. It's the corpse of officer J.D. Tippit surgically altered to look like the President.

On arriving home Liggett was informed the plot was in serious trouble. His wife Lois told how he staggered in the door unkempt, dishevelled, and quite obviously exhausted; which was very out of character for a man who took pride in always being neat, tidy and organized.

Minutes later they were speeding down the highway towards Corpus Christi, utterly bewildered as to what was going on?

Chain-smoking at the wheel Liggett was looking increasingly nervous. It wasn't just that his botched reconstruction had

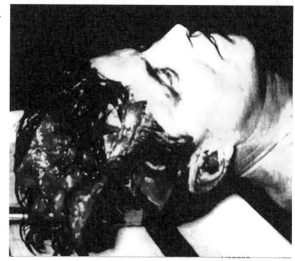

failed to convince and would lead to courtroom testimony of bullets doing u-turns inside the President's head.

The problem was that the Patsy was still alive.

Deputy sheriff Roger Craig told investigators it was plain to him that Lee Harvey Oswald was not meant to survive his arrest procedure. He said that when he arrived at the Texas Theatre a group of his fellow officers were waiting at the rear guns drawn, and that it was quite obvious that Oswald was meant to make a break out the back door where he would run into a hail of gunfire.

However Oswald himself was an intelligence agent, and once he realized he had been chosen as the fall guy he briefly prolonged his existence by loudly yelling, so that all the witnesses present could hear, I am *not* resisting arrest! I am *not* resisting arrest!

This is why Liggett, like all the others involved in the plot, was shaking in his boots on November 23rd. They were all aware that a sharp lawyer could get Oswald released simply by discovering that the chain of evidence had been broken in relation to Kennedy's remains. Once free to talk, and with intimate knowledge of the major players in the assassination plot, he could have gotten the heads of the FBI and CIA all the military chiefs of staff, the Mafia Chieftains and the Dallas oilmen all thrown in jail together for murder.

Extract from TV interview with Lois Liggett

MRS LIGGETT: It was about 24 hours before I heard from him. He came home, and he walked in the door, and when I saw him he physically looked like he had really been through a very traumatic experience. His clothes were disarrayed; and that was so out of character for him. And he said we're going to get out of town for a while until all of this blows over. That was a quote, because I thought well, what blows over??

Many people have wondered how the plotters could be so unbelievably dumb? and so unbelievably obvious, as to have Oswald murdered Live on national television?

The simple truth was that they had absolutely no choice.

Their botched assassination attempt had proved that they were not as smart as they thought they were. The actual shooting had gone very badly. Most of the shots had missed. They'd had to botch the autopsy, and now they were having to botch the silencing of the patsy.

Lois Liggett recalled that the moment Ruby fired the atmosphere in their motel room evaporated.

The family turned around and went straight back home to discover that Mr. Liggett now enjoyed a new vocation. It appeared he had suddenly come into millions, which bought his family a big new house and himself a new lifestyle which included many wild poker parties at which among others he hosted David Ferrie.

This was not Lois Liggett's scene. She divorced him, heard that not long afterwards he was arrested for murder, and then shot dead while trying to escape. But this was not the end of Liggett's story.

His new wife told Lois that the man she buried could not have been John Melvin Liggett because the corpse she was shown had a moustache and he couldn't grow one. Then, many years later Lois Liggett actually saw her deceased ex-husband, in a casino, while on a trip to Las Vegas. Quite clearly this man had been the beneficiary of yet another CIA body switch, and to this day doubts remain as to the true fate of Jack Ruby, Lee Oswald, John Liggett and, the President himself.

Many researchers now believe the plotters may have kept Kennedy's remains as a souvenir, and buried J.D. Tippit in Arlington Cemetery.

All added together the pilots, spotters, radio men, Mafia assassins, embalmers, physicians and corrupt agents from the FBI, CIA and Dallas police had cost the American Nazis 25 million dollars: approximately two Billion in today's money.

But they could afford it. In the years that followed they cynically kept the war in Vietnam going by putting in just enough troops so the line never moved forward or back, and while the American fat cats grew fatter on military industrial conflicts their Mafia friends used the CIA's complete immunity to smuggle trillions of dollars worth of cocaine and heroin around the world.

Deborah Godwin
(Liggett's step-daughter)

MRS LIGGETT: The minute he saw that he looked at me and said: "everything's okay now" And you could just see his face. He was like, all the pressure had been taken off of him. MRS LIGGETT'S DAUGHTER: All of a sudden he was like, sigh of relief, let's go. We can go home now. It was basically pack your things come on we're leaving, you know? Now we can go.

Sarah McClendon

Extract from an exchange during a Televised White House Briefing between Clinton and McClendon

McCLENDON: Sir, the Republicans are trying to blame you for the existence of a small air base at Mena Arkansas. This base was set up by George Bush and Oliver North and the CIA to help the Iran Contras, and they brought in plane load after plane load of Cocaine there for sale in the United States and then they took the money and bought weapons and took them back to the Contras all of which is illegal as you know under the Boland act: but tell me, did they tell you that this had to be in existence because of National Security?
CLINTON: Well, let me answer the question. No they didn't tell me anything about it.

Of course when criminals are making easy money they tend to become lazy and careless, and this is what led to.. Watergate.

When the two plainclothes police officers switched the lights on in the Watergate building, who should they find hiding there? Frank Sturgis and Bernard Barker, who were working for E. Howard Hunt: exactly the same people who had murdered President Kennedy nine years earlier.

Frank Sturgis and Bernard Barker (1960)

Sturgis even told the *San Francisco Chronicle* that the true reason for their burglary of the Watergate offices was to retrieve compromising pictures of CIA men in Dealey Plaza which the Democrats were going to have published.

Of course somebody had to take a fall for conducting such a woefully sloppy operation, and when Howard Hunt found himself in prison for 33 months he rather turned against his old friends for making him into the Patsy on this occasion.

Frank Sturgis and Bernard Barker (1972)

He began sending messages to President Richard Nixon that he might just tell all he knew about what really happened in Dallas on November 22nd 1963, and one of Nixon's presidential aides, Dean Birch, recalls that when he heard about this George Bush "broke out all over in assholes and shit himself to death."

It was this situation which led directly to what journalists now refer to as the "Watergate Murder" the crash of flight 553.

On December the 8th 1972 Dorothy Wetzel Hunt, the wife of E. Howard Hunt, boarded a flight from Washington to Chicago: a CIA agent like her husband she carried a quarter of a million dollars in her bag

Dorothy Hunt

which was to buy the silence of his Watergate co-conspirators. Travelling along with Dorothy was CBS News correspondent Michelle Clark, whose CIA boyfriend had been able to give her a unique journalistic insight into what Watergate was really all about.

Michelle Clark

These two women boarded the aircraft with a dozen other individuals who at that time had information which E. Howard Hunt claimed was going "to blow the White House out of the water."

As the plane made its final approach through fog and very low cloud the people living near the aircraft runway sensed something rather strange was going on. The normally quiet suburban street suddenly filled up with cars: and a moment later, having been told to power down too early, Flight 553 emerged from the mist and clipped the branches of some trees before crashing on top of several bungalows on West 7070 Street.

The watching neighbours were then staggered to see FBI agents immediately leap out of their cars and start rooting around in the debris a full ten minutes before the fire brigade even arrived on the scene.

Forty-four people, including Dorothy Hunt and Michelle Clark, were killed in the crash.

E. Howard Hunt served his time and came out of prison a widower, and a million dollars richer.

The Nazi shadow government of the United States had faced a blackmail threat and the possibility that their complicity in the murder of President Kennedy might become public knowledge.

Their response was to bring down a civilian airliner onto a residential district. They covered it up by having FBI agents on the ground seek out and remove all incriminating documents from the dead bodies found in the wreckage, and when the local TV station received an anonymous phone call from a

radio ham who had monitored the deliberately misleading exchanges from the Midway control tower which caused Flight 553 to crash an FBI agent simply confiscated all the tapes, thus eradicating all information pertaining to the "accident."

This is how the agents of the U.S. government now behave.

They function essentially as a goon squad of mercenaries and murderers hardly any different to Hitler's Gestapo: and they are used as a private intelligence service, and as personal hit-men, for America's richest families, their only role being to cover up the dirty tricks which the rich people are playing on their fellow countrymen every day.

Along with threats and murder the most important weapon used by this private army of foot-pads in this ongoing cover-up is disinformation: and it's here that we can now address the question which will probably be bothering the huge numbers of people who have taken an interest in the Kennedy assassination, and in the many documentaries produced by assassination researchers over the years. What happened to Badgeman?

The answer is very simple. He never existed. He was simply a phantom created by the CIA's disinformation machine to lay down a trail which led nowhere.

So now another question appears. If this is so, why have so many people spent a quarter of a century trying to discover his identity?

By examining this question it is now possible to reveal the extraordinary lengths America's rulers have gone to in order to hide the truth about the Kennedy assassination.

America's oligarchs grossly underestimated the courage and skill of those who tried to uncover the truth about the Kennedy killing.

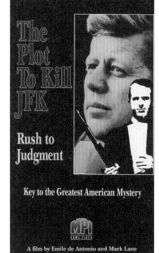

None more so than the brilliant and tenacious Mark Lane. By the mid-1960s his film *Rush to Judgement* had left the country in no doubt that there had been multiple gunmen acting together in some sort of conspiracy. Once he had proved this beyond any doubt the only question remaining was: how big was the conspiracy? So it came as no surprise when polls started showing that nine out of ten Americans believed it had to be the CIA

This internal memorandum (right) reveals just how nervous the agency was about this development. It spells out in no uncertain terms the concern spreading in the corridors of power, and the urgent need to rectify this situation through the use of "assets in the media."

Dp of 1035-960

DISPATCH

	CLASSIFICATION	PROCESSING ACTION
	SECRET	MARKED FOR INDEXING
TO Chiefs, Certain Stations and Bases		X NO INDEXING REQUIRED
INFO.		ONLY QUALIFIED DESK
		CAN JUDGE INDEXING
FROM Chief, WOVIEW		MICROFILM
SUBJECT Countering Criticism of the Warren Report		

ACTION REQUIRED - REFERENCES

PAUL H. FOR OSWALD FILES & COPIES PSYCH — *THIS WAS PULLED TOGETHER BY OF CA STAFF IN CLOSE CONJUNCTION WITH CI/R&A. WE FURNISHED MOST OF THE SOURCE MATERIAL, PROVIDED SOME OF THE THEMES, AND PROVIDED GENERAL "EXPERTISE" ON THE CASE. THIS SPECIFIC ARTICLE WAS WRITTEN BY*

1. **Our Concern.** From the day of President Kennedy's assassination on, there has been speculation about the responsibility for his murder. Although this was stemmed for a time by the Warren Commission report (which appeared at the end of September 1964), various writers have now had time to scan the Commission's published report and documents for new pretexts for questioning, and there has been a new wave of books and articles criticizing the Commission's findings. In most cases the critics have speculated as to the existence of some kind of conspiracy, and often they have implied that the Commission itself was involved. Presumably as a result of the increasing challenge to the Warren Commission's Report, a public opinion poll recently indicated that 46% of the American public did not think that Oswald acted alone, while more than half of those polled thought that the Commission had left some questions unresolved. Doubtless polls abroad would show similar, or possibly more adverse, results.

2. This trend of opinion is a matter of concern to the U.S. government, including our organization. The members of the Warren Commission were naturally chosen for their integrity, experience, and prominence. They represented both major parties, and they and their staff were deliberately drawn from all sections of the country. Just because of the standing of the Commissioners, efforts to impugn their rectitude and wisdom tend to cast doubt on the whole leadership of American society. Moreover, there seems to be an increasing tendency to hint that President Johnson himself, as the one person who might be said to have benefited, was in some way responsible for the assassination. Innuendo of such seriousness affects not only the individual concerned, but also the whole reputation of the American government. Our organization itself is directly involved: among other facts, we contributed information to the investigation. Conspiracy theories have frequently thrown suspicion on our organization, for example by falsely alleging that Lee Harvey Oswald worked for us. The aim of this dispatch is to provide material for countering and discrediting the claims of the conspiracy theorists, so as to inhibit the circulation of such claims in other countries. Background information is supplied in a classified section and in a number of unclassified attachments.

3. **Action.** We do not recommend that discussion of the assassination question be initiated where it is not already taking place. Where discussion is active, however, addressees are requested:

		BD COPY	201-289.248
CROSS REFERENCE X INDEX	DISPATCH SYMBOL AND NUMBER		DATE
9 attachments h/w	BD 5847		4/1/67
SECRET	CLASSIFICATION	NOS FILE NUMBER	
Unclassified	SECRET	DESTROY WHEN NO LONGER NEEDED	

**CIA HISTORICAL REVIEW PROGRAM
RELEASE IN FULL 1998**

CONTINUATION OF DISPATCH	CLASSIFICATION SECRET	DISPATCH SYMBOL AND NUMBER BD 5847

a. To discuss the publicity problem with liaison and friendly elite contacts (especially politicians and editors), pointing out that the Warren Commission made as thorough an investigation as humanly possible, that the charges of the critics are without serious foundation, and that further speculative discussion only plays into the hands of the opposition. Point out also that parts of the conspiracy talk appear to be deliberately generated by Communist propagandists. Urge them to use their influence to discourage unfounded and irresponsible speculation.

b. To employ propaganda assets to answer and refute the attacks of the critics. Book reviews and feature articles are particularly appropriate for this purpose. The unclassified attachments to this guidance should provide useful background material for passage to assets. Our play should point out, as applicable, that the critics are (i) wedded to theories adopted before the evidence was in, (ii) politically interested, (iii) financially interested, (iv) hasty and inaccurate in their research, or (v) infatuated with their own theories. In the course of discussions of the whole phenomenon of criticism, a useful strategy may be to single out Epstein's theory for attack, using the attached Fletcher Knebel article and Spectator piece for background. (Although Mark Lane's book is much less convincing than Epstein's and comes off badly where contested by knowledgeable critics, it is also much more difficult to answer as a whole, as one becomes lost in a morass of unrelated details.)

4. In private or media discussion not directed at any particular writer, or in attacking publications which may be yet forthcoming, the following arguments should be useful:

a. No significant new evidence has emerged which the Commission did not consider. The assassination is sometimes compared (e.g., by Joachim Joesten and Bertrand Russell) with the Dreyfus case; however, unlike that case, the attacks on the Warren Commission have produced no new evidence, no new culprits have been convincingly identified, and there is no agreement among the critics. (A better parallel, though an imperfect one, might be with the Reichstag fire of 1933, which some competent historians (Fritz Tobias, A.J.P. Taylor, D.C. Watt) now believe was set by Van der Lubbe on his own initiative, without acting for either Nazis or Communists; the Nazis tried to pin the blame on the Communists, but the latter have been much more successful in convincing the world that the Nazis were to blame.)

b. Critics usually overvalue particular items and ignore others. They tend to place more emphasis on the recollections of individual eyewitnesses (which are less reliable and more divergent -- and hence offer more hand-holds for criticism) and less on ballistic, autopsy, and photographic evidence. A close examination of the Commission's records will usually show that the conflicting eyewitness accounts are quoted out of context, or were discarded by the Commission for good and sufficient reason.

c. Conspiracy on the large scale often suggested would be impossible to conceal in the United States, esp. since informants could expect to receive large royalties, etc. Note that Robert Kennedy, Attorney General at the time and John F. Kennedy's brother, would be the last man to overlook or conceal any conspiracy. And as one reviewer pointed out, Congressman Gerald R. Ford would hardly have held his tongue for the sake of the Democratic administration, and Senator Russell would have had every political interest in exposing any misdeeds on the part of Chief Justice Warren. A conspirator moreover would hardly choose a location for a shooting where so much depended on conditions beyond his control: the route, the speed of the cars, the moving target, the risk that the assassin would be discovered. A group of wealthy conspirators could have arranged much more secure conditions.

d. Critics have often been enticed by a form of intellectual pride: they light on some theory and fall in love with it; they also scoff at the Commission because it did not always answer every question with a flat decision one way or the other. Actually, the make-up of the Commission and its staff was an excellent safeguard against over-commitment to any one theory, or against the illicit transformation of probabilities into certainties.

FORM 53a 8-64	USE PREVIOUS EDITION.	CLASSIFICATION SECRET	X CONTINUED	PAGE NO. TWO

This great image problem led America's Nazis into initiating Operation Mockingbird, an ongoing policy of using the colossal wealth they were now amassing from drugs and weapons sales to buy up as many TV and film companies, newspapers and local and national radio stations as they could lay their hands on, to the point where by the 1970's they were proudly boasting that "everyone of any significance in the media is CIA."

Virtually every well-known journalist, newspaper editor, and television presenter became a secret CIA agent, as did many entertainers and film stars. The question now was how best to use trusted public figures like Walter Cronkite, and this was how the first investigative documentaries about the Kennedy assassination came to be made.

Extract from the televised Frank Church House Intelligence Committee hearings

CHAIRMAN: Do you have any people being paid by the CIA who are contributing to a major circulation American Journal?

CIA SPOKESMAN: We do have people who submit pieces to American journals.

CHAIRMAN: Do you have any people paid by the CIA who are working for television networks?

CIA SPOKESMAN: This I think gets into the kind of details mister chairman that I'd like to get into in executive session.

It will come as a terrific shock to those who have sought truth and solace in these many films, feature articles and TV specials to learn that every last one of them, including Oliver Stone's *JFK*, was actually produced by the CIA.

A classic early example of this kind of disinformation was the Nova Film which featured two scientists: Brian Holstrom and Steve Isabel, who found BadgeMan in a tiny fragment of the famous Mary Moorman Polaroid through photographic enhancement.

But when investigators took the trouble to actually measure the size of these three figures it became obvious that they were so tiny they were too small to even be children.

Using the scale provided by Abraham Zapruder over on the right it's clear that these alleged people are so lacking in stature they wouldn't actually have been able to look over the stockade fence.

The truth is that they never existed; so the question now is, who were Holstrom and Isabel? and who for that matter was Gordon Arnold? the old-age pensioner who appeared in *The Men Who Killed Kennedy* to claim that badge-man had kicked him and taken his camera?

The answer is that they were all professional actors, because this is how the Devil operates. Devils mix lies with truth in order to make the lies sound more plausible, and it seems that the idea for using actors in this way might very likely have come from E. Howard Hunt himself.

After Hunt's deathbed confession in which he admitted the involvement of the CIA his son Saint John Hunt posted many revealing statements about what kind of character his father was. It's quite well known that E. Howard Hunt wrote spy novels and screenplays, and when he was discussing this Saint John Hunt maintained his father tried to live his life as if every day was another exciting scene from a movie, to the total exclusion of his own family.

Gordon Arnold

The way Saint John Hunt put it was "he would never cut carrots or go shopping with us or anything like that … James Bond doesn't have a family"

Historians are well aware that the CIA studies everything which is impressive, and it now seems very plain that they were greatly influenced by the brilliance of the Levinson & Link *Columbo* series: particularly one episode "Murder, Smoke and Shadows" in which the killer, who is a ruthless young movie director, tries to confuse and mislead Columbo through his powers of creating illusion, only to have the table's turned when this is done back to him – because the whole point of that episode is that the audience never know who is and who isn't supposed to be an actor.

The Men Who Killed Kennedy series was laid out in the same way. Whilst a few of the interviewees, like the Willis family, were genuine, most of the people claiming to be witnesses were simply actors whose only job was to keep people's minds on the grassy knoll so they would never think about the storm drains and where the shots actually originated. Oliver Stone's film was made to serve exactly the same purpose.

It's also very clear that the CIA spent a lot of time studying the emotional breakdown in interviews with people like the ambulance driver Aubrey Rike.

Intelligence agents are   all aware that when an audience see someone sobbing from grief on screen they tend to become emotional themselves. This is how sensitive, humane people react, and when this happens you're no longer thinking.

And when you're no longer thinking critically, when you suspend skepticism for the sake of emotionalism, you can be fooled.

Of course having heard this people will wonder how anyone could be cynical to such a degree? and it's a perfectly legitimate question, because, as we shall see later, this would not be the last time that the American public were fooled by actors sobbing on national TV. And these monstrous fabrications were not confined only to Television.

In 2003 a book was published called *Blood, Money And Power*. Ostensibly written by Texas law attorney Barr McClellan this book signalled a shift in establishment policy by claiming that Lyndon Baines Johnson, a natural suspect as the king who might have killed the king, was behind the entire plot and used his own attorney Ed Clark to pay off the gunman.

Researchers noticed that at exactly the same time a lot of information suddenly became available about all the murder plots LBJ had been involved in with Cliff Carter and Billy Sol Estes.

We were then treated to the sensational deathbed confession of E. Howard Hunt, and in the book itself the serious researchers found this extraordinary paragraph:

Wallace centred on Kennedy's head and fired. The shot went almost 200 feet but was barely low and slightly to the right, hitting the

Cliff Carter   Billy Sol Estes

President in the back shoulder blade. The bullet was deflected upward ever so slightly exiting at the tie-knot: the bullet's jacket separating to hit and crack the windshield, the remaining slug hitting the kerbing in front of James Tague, an onlooker standing in front of the triple underpass on Commerce Street. The slug knocked cement shards in all directions. A splinter nicked Tague on the cheek.

So just exactly what is going on here?

This is quite obviously a ludicrous assertion, so what is it all about?

What it's all about is that the CIA actually wrote this book. They knew that the critics had been able to laugh loud and long at the single bullet theory because the FBI had had to change their story. At first they'd accepted the indisputable evidence that James Tague was scratched by a bullet as he watched from below the overpass because they initially claimed that the first shot alone had gone through the President and the Governor, making seven separate wounds in two different men. The second shot was the head shot, and presumably the third struck Tague.

However once the Zapruder film and dozens of eye witnesses made it plain the first shot missed the FBI had a problem. How could they account for the throat shot, head shot, and Tague shot with just two remaining bullets?

This utterly ridiculous paragraph was a lame attempt, after forty years, to come up with an answer. And the lengths the CIA went to, to get people to believe it, were contrived to say the least.

Its first of all the simplest matter to refute this version of events by asking how the CIA could possibly know this is how it happened? The bullets splitting apart in mid-air? Are they saying they had Dealey

Plaza rigged with fast-motion cameras which allowed them to replay the flight of every bullet in slow motion?? If so, we'd all love to see those pictures!

And even more to this, Barr McClellan's interview became the linchpin in the final episode of *The Men Who Killed Kennedy* which was then banned from public broadcasting after a lawsuit was allegedly brought against the History Channel by former Presidents Carter and Ford, and their friends Jack Valenti, Bill Moyers and Lady Bird Johnson.

Of course this was just more disinformation. What the plotters hoped to achieve was that by getting the series banned, but making it available on the Internet, the seekers after truth would be duped into thinking it must be true precisely because it was being banned from mainstream media. It's a double-bluff.

It is quite possible after all of this ludicrous skulduggery that even the CIA themselves couldn't remember what purpose it was all supposed to serve, but the general idea was that the public was supposed to swallow the notion that Lyndon Baines Johnson was the primary culprit in this entire affair, because he's dead and can't speak for himself.

Extract from a TV interview with Lyndon Baines Johnson during the period of his premiership which was never Broadcast

PRESIDENT JOHNSON: I can't honestly say that I've ever been completely relieved of the fact that there might have been international connections. (i.e. involved in the Kennedy assassination)

TV INTERVIEWER: You mean you still feel that there might have been?

PRESIDENT JOHNSON: Well, I have not completely discounted it.

It is absolute nonsense to suggest any such thing.

Lyndon Baines Johnson was, like Hitler and Richard Nixon, a mere puppet of the oilmen and the merchant bankers and military industrialists; something he finally admitted to: The notion that he was the criminal mastermind behind the Kennedy assassination is simply another disinformation falsehood dreamed up by the CIA He was most definitely involved in the plot, and offered up his personal hit-man Malcom Wallace to be part of it, but the men who actually masterminded the plot were Allen Dulles and David Atlee Phillips, with George Bush being the most important figure in the actual execution of the plan; and even they, in the end, proved themselves to be just as crude and obvious as anyone else in the way they took care of anyone who might incriminate them.

On the 22nd of February 1967 Eladio del Valle and David Ferrie were both murdered within minutes of each other when it seemed they might give information to the Jim Garrison investigation.

Charles Voyd Harrelson and Milwaukee Phil Alderisio suffered convenient early deaths in jail; and having been ordered to testify before the House Select Committee on assassinations both Charles Nicoletti and George de Mohrenschildt were shot dead at exactly the same time on the 29th of March 1977.

Having being scheduled to testify before the same committee Johnny Roselli met a similar fate.

His body was found floating in an oil drum in Dumbfounding Bay Miami, just after Malcolm Wallace was murdered in exactly the same way as Lee Bowers. On a stretch of empty American highway his car was forced off the road and CIA agents smashed his head into the steering wheel until he died to make it appear like a single car accident.

Not long afterwards Sam Giancana was shot in the back of the head while cooking sausages, and his spy inside the Chicago police force, Richard Cain, was blasted to death with a sawn-off shotgun in Rose's Sandwich Shop on the 19th of December 1973.

Absolute proof that George H.W. Bush was the most important figure behind these grisly murders and the Kennedy assassination surfaced quite recently in a Declassified FBI memo which revealed he was working for the CIA in 1963, and not from 1977 onwards as he'd always claimed.

He had been a lifelong friend of George de Mohrenschildt, who had actually begged him for help when he realized the CIA were trying to kill him.

It was therefore rather ironic that when the police checked de Mohrenschildt's wallet they found an address card which gave them a direct lead straight to the guilty party had they but chosen to follow it up. It said George "Poppy" Bush (his CIA code name) Zapata Petroleum Midland Texas.

Ferrie

del Valle

de Mohrenschildt

Giancana

It became a farewell note from the man who coordinated the crime of the century; a man whose father Prescott Bush had created the CIA in the first place, along with his friends some 30 years before, purely in order to take care of their own business interests.

They arrogantly believed they were more intelligent than anyone, but in the end the means that the George Bush-led CIA chose to silence all the major underworld figures who might incriminate them proved to be every bit as crude and obvious as Ruby's killing of Oswald on Television.

The whole point of George Bush and his Central Intelligence Agency was that they were supposed to be intelligent, and yet, in the end, they couldn't even fool little old ladies.

Extract from a Television street-interview with a savvy American Lady of great experience who has seen it all

Old-Age Pensioner: Who's going to inhibit them?? The gangsters that are running this country is going to inhibit somebody??

All institutions of the American government are essentially a gangster syndicate.

And everybody knows this.

So perhaps it's time now to ask what we have learned? and how best we can use this new understanding about the West's secret history to evaluate what is really going on in our world right now?

To begin with, let's answer a couple of questions which have perplexed many people over the years.

A great many researchers and historians have wondered why the Kennedy family themselves almost seemed to be aiding and abetting the cover-up by choosing to be so quiet about the assassination itself after the revelations of Chuck Giancana? There now seems little doubt that this is because they know a full disclosure of Joe Kennedy's dirty political dealings with the Mafia would likely leave the Kennedy name in a very tarnished state. Up until now history has tended to give the Kennedy patriarch a distinguished and squeaky clean image which went along with his appointment as the American ambassador to Britain. Like most things about the ruling class this image is false, because it's clear that Joe Kennedy was every bit as big a crook as his business associate Sam Giancana.

Kopechne

However it also seems necessary now to revise the entire history of the Kennedy brothers. The reputation of Edward Kennedy never recovered from the Chappaquiddick incident in which Mary Jo Kopechne lost her life when she drowned in his overturned car when he allegedly drove off an unlit bridge whilst under the influence.

At the time the public believed this was a married man misbehaving, but it's come to light recently that our old friends Frank Sturgis and E. Howard Hunt were seen in the Martha's Vineyard area just prior to the "accident." Once again it's the same dirty people pulling the same dirty tricks.

The media's treatment of this affair destroyed any chance Edward Kennedy might have had of becoming President, and we do now have to wonder if this was yet another example of the CIA controlling public opinion?

To the same end it is also now clear why such venerable institutions as the BBC and other prominent European Broadcasters have assisted in the cover-up.

They always knew the Kennedy assassination was a can of worms; and that if the whole truth in the story were pursued vigorously it would lead right back to the gates of Auschwitz, and the obscene profits which Europe's royalty and heads of state made from their investments in slave labour.

This is a brutal truth which the West must now confront.

And an equally brutal problem the United States must now face is the question of what has happened to the U.S. military in the intervening years since it murdered its own commander-in-chief? The answer is that America's armed forces are now completely controlled by the American Mafia. The mob don't even need hit-men anymore; they use United States Marines as assassins. They are, as Sam Giancana

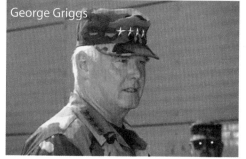

George Griggs

said, one organization, who keep a low profile while they control the entire world as a business. And in an effort to prove this is so in 1998 Pastor Rick Straw-Cutter videotaped a quite remarkable interview with Kay Pollard Griggs: formerly the wife of Colonel George Griggs, who for many years was assigned to NATO.

He was also an alcoholic of that well-known kind who are shy and unable to communicate when they are sober but who then cannot stop talking once they have a drink.

During the course of a stormy marriage punctuated by periods of domestic violence which cost Kay Griggs many black eyes and broken bones she learned that her husband had been turned into a brutal psychopath as a consequence of his military training, which included induction into what is known as the "Pink Triangle: the Cherry Marines."

Over the years far too much has been written about Lee Harvey Oswald, but what is remarkable is that few historians were ever aware that like most Marines who worked in intelligence he was homosexually recruited, and was part of the same-sex club which included Jack Ruby, George Senator and David Ferrie.

Kay Griggs explains that these selection procedures came into the U.S. military when the cream of the death's-head sporting Nazi top-brass joined the American ranks at the war's end. Ever since then the Greek and Spartan traditions which Hitler so admired, and which were integral to the German army, have found their way into American military culture, and are now manifest in the way that the old skull and bones procedure for identifying and most importantly controlling rising stars is now used to select the top brass of the future. In a nutshell, boy soldiers who want to rise in the ranks can only do so by doing 'favours' for the older men.

This is how military recruits are now controlled, and the Mafia military exert a similar hold over all career politicians. At some time on the way up they are manoeuvred into a compromising position: usually through the use of two-way mirrors in a brothel; and once the mafia military have got something on them the career politicians, judges, senior police officers and media moguls face a stark choice. Either take your payoff, which is usually worth millions of dollars, or go to jail, for life, for your misdemeanour.

It is with these kinds of tactics, first used by Sam Giancana in the 1930's, that what are now known as the five Mafia families of the New York metropolitan area, the Genovese, Gambino, Luchesse, Colombo and the Bonanno control all politics in the United States, and through their business arrangements with the five-star generals and CIA control all cocaine and heroin trafficking throughout the entire world.

After the dust had settled on the Kennedy assassination Sam Giancana explained to his younger brother that the mob and the CIA had "taken care of JFK together" because they were essentially "two sides of the same coin." In the last 50 years that relationship between these two secret societies has become even closer, to the point where they are now indistinguishable.

The people who live in the third world are so well aware of what is really going on they have come to call the CIA the cocaine importing agency.

The World Wide Web now abounds with proof to back this up and although many people were skeptical at first about Kay Griggs, in recent times her most sensational claims have been fully endorsed by the FBI chief Ted Gundersen, who gave several interviews in support.

Extract from a TV interview between Kay Griggs and Pastor Rick Straw-Cutter

STRAW-CUTTER: So George Bush, and all these people, rise up through the ranks, and they're all in the same Club. No wonder.. you know I saw a little TV clip one time where a reporter was asking George Bush and others about the order of the skull and bones.. (extract from a TV interview of George Bush during his premiership by NBC anchor Tim Russert who suffered an unexpected heart-attack soon afterwards)

RUSSERT: You were both in Skull and Bones, the secret society?

PRESIDENT BUSH: It's so secret we can't talk about it.

RUSSERT: What does that mean for America?

STRAW-CUTTER: I mean if this really got out that these guys are all inducted because they've got some kind of homosexual thing on them!

GRIGGS: Right! indoctrination, I mean induction.. they have to do that, they do that in a coffin, and it's even now coming into the military totally, the Chiefs do that, they put them in the coffin: they do the bowling ball trick.

STRAW-CUTTER: Okay you're going to have to explain this, what happens when you get in the coffin? why do you get in a coffin??

GRIGGS: When you get your Eagles, that's a German thing okay? It's what the German High Command did, and most of them you know? had the boyfriends and stuff? the croups and all of that. It's a German thing that they say goes back to Ancient Greece, and it's all the male, marine-looking men that they they do it with. So now the Chiefs have to do that … what they do is they get … George said, it's like a zoo.. they they get everybody really drunk.. and they sometimes call it dining-in; Shell-back is another time that they do it: not everybody does it, but the ones who do it, if they're young, they get right up to the top.

STRAW-CUTTER: Okay so what actually do they do? they've got a coffin...?

GRIGGS: Anal sex. In the coffin.

What is basically happening is that the United States military use Air Force bases in Europe to connect with the third world: particularly Pakistan and Afghanistan, where the poppy fields are cultivated. This is the real reason for the conflict in Afghanistan; it's to protect the record harvests of heroin which almost ended when the Taliban took power – but they don't tell the soldiers this. And it's a truth you'll never hear on NBC or BBC.

Having brought the refined cocaine and heroin into Europe and the United States, it is then passed on to the Mafia for sale at street level, sometimes by police officers in uniform.

It's an arrangement which Nets the generals and the Mafia Chiefs Billions – and the fact that someone of Ted Gundersen's credibility was completely ignored when he went public with this information underlines the fact that our entire mainstream media, as well as the entire justice system, has been bought off.

So the question must now be asked, if this shadow government, of the world's only super-state, can get away with the murder of a President and, through their wealth, be in total control of the United States military, media, and the justice system; what else might they be getting away with?

Extract from a TV interview with Ted Gundersen

GUNDERSEN: This cult was involved in distributing drugs up and down the East Coast. Drugs that were being flown in from Southeast Asia in military planes. The operation was by certain army personnel and also CIA she told me that there were generals involved in the drug operation; there were police officers, and at least two attorneys in the Fayetteville North Carolina area. The path that this led me down is mind boggling. Over the last 23, 24 years I have developed so much information about the situation as it exists in our great country, and gone public with it as much as possible, and yet I am being ignored.

Could it possibly be that the serious researchers have been right all along? and, remembering what happened to Flight 553, that 9/11 truly was one huge confidence trick?

Once the dust had settled on 9/11 people immediately began to realize there was something very wrong with the 9/11 TV coverage. First along came Dylan Avery with his amazing film *Loose Change*.

He proved conclusively that the official report was nonsense because aircraft fuel does not burn at even half the temperature required to melt steel; and that the towers defied the laws of physics by collapsing, with perfect uniformity, at free-fall speed.

Buildings in Germany which were bombed over and over again didn't collapse with perfect uniformity down to ground level.

Avery also pointed out that in Kennedy's time his Chiefs of Staff drafted plans to kill innocent people and commit acts of terrorism in the United States order to whip up support for a war with Cuba: code-named Operation Northwoods.

These plans included "hijacking planes and blowing up ships and landmark buildings" in order to stimulate "a helpful wave of national indignation which could be used to oust Fidel Castro."

And there wasn't anything exceptional in this initiative.

Northwoods was an offshoot of the notorious Operation Gladio, a sustained campaign organized by MI6 and the CIA which perpetrated many bombing atrocities in post-war Europe which they blamed on what they said were communists terror organizations.

A typical example was the horrific bombing of Bologna railway station in 1980.

Italians will be appalled to learn this outrage was committed by the Americans and the British, but this particular atrocity, which, like all others during this period, was intended to keep people living in fear of a bogus enemy so they would accept increasing state control by so-called strong leaders, illustrates only too well the fact that some forty years prior to 9/11 the cabal of secret Nazis who killed Kennedy were making serious preparations for terrorist attacks upon their European allies and even upon their own country.

In the 9/11 news footage it is abundantly clear that the interviewees are actually paid actors speaking lines which have been written for them.

This is exactly the same situation as in *The Men Who Killed Kennedy* and because these are people who are being expected to perform? they tend to overdo it.

It is perfectly clear that the 9/11 Street people are trying much too hard to convince their audience.

Extract from street interview with paid actor on 9/11

PAID ACTOR: I feel like I was in a movie!

Extract from *The Men Who Killed Kennedy* in which the actor playing Gordon Arnold suffers from a very bad case of over-acting

ARNOLD: "I could be only one … (shaking) who saw the man.. he killed the President … (sobbing) and to be honest with you. if I'd have known this.… I wouldn't have given the interview"

Who really talks like this?

9/11 was in reality just another CIA special effects movie production; and it really has become the Kennedy assassinations' long-lost twin, because witnesses who know the truth of what really happened are all being murdered.

This didn't stop some people from immediately pointing out that the London Tube bombings were a hoax. The alleged terrorists couldn't have ridden into London on a train which was cancelled and seasoned researchers are now becoming quite surprised and how sloppy and obvious these alleged 'terrorist' acts are becoming.

Any detective would instantly realize

Extract from what most researchers believed was the most spurious 911 witness interview with a man dubbed the "Harley Guy" who "spoke like an infomercial actor"

HARLEY GUY: Approximately several minutes after the first plane had hit I saw this plane come out of nowhere and just scream right into the side of the Twin Towers, exploding through the other side, and then I witnessed both towers collapse, one first and then the second, mostly due to structural failure, because the fire was just too intense.

```
X-Mailer: Internet Mail Service (5.5.2657.72)
Content-Type: multipart/alternative;
boundary="----_=_NextPart_001_01C5A979.682BB90C"
X-Antivirus: AVG for E-mail 7.0.344 [267.10.17]

------_=_NextPart_001_01C5A979.682BB900
Content-Type: text/plain

Dear Nick

The information you require is as follows:
```

Booked departure time	Actual departure time	Arrival time at King's Cross Thameslink
07.16	07.21	08.19
07.20	On time	08.15
07.24	07.25	08.23
07.30	07.42	08.39
07.40	Cancelled	n/a
07.48	07.56	08.42

Kind regards

Chris Hudson
Communications Manager
Thameslink Rail Limited

the Woolwich terror incident was a joke. We were shown pictures of a supposedly decapitated man lying prone on the street: if that were true he should be lying in a puddle of his own blood, and the alleged attacker would be soaked in blood all over his front from arterial spray.

All terrorism is fake.

It is military deception practised by the rich upon the poor in an ongoing class war, and the most important weapon at their disposal in this class war are Television presenters.

The BBC has actually become the Ministry of truth from Orwell's *1984*.

Everyone working for the BBC today is a whore of the ruling class and a traitor to our way of life, because it is very hard to believe they are all unwitting accomplices in this class war. When we remember that it was some of the BBC's own journalists who revealed that the 9/11 hijackers were all alive it's hard to accept that their news presenter colleagues haven't figured out the totalitarian nature of what people like Jane Standley, who reported the collapse of World Trade Centre 7 twenty minutes before it came down, are really up to.

And yet still they go on giving us reassuring smiles, while telling lies; on behalf of the ruling class. Of course then people ask oh yes yes yes but why would they do it? Why is all of this Muslim, multi-cultural, political correctness thing happening to us right now? It's happening because we no longer have an enemy.

Tourists today can visit what used to be the Eastern Bloc, and they can photograph the derelict, rusting heap of scrap-metal which used to be the Soviet war machine. It has gone.

And this has created an unprecedented political situation which the world has never seen before in which there is only one super-state: the Anglo-American alliance.

No other power on earth today is capable of fighting a war on the grand scale: China, North Korea, Russia, simply do not have the economic resources. So in order to make us believe we still have an enemy, and therefore have to live in fear, the rich had to provide us with a new enemy, and this is why in recent years they've encouraged unstable Islamic people to emigrate to the West. It's to provide us with a ready-made enemy.

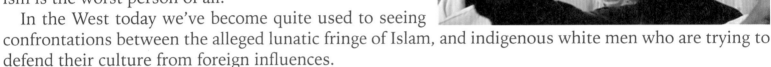

This is their master plan for this single-super state age.

And it's for this reason that they perverted political correctness to make people believe that anybody who refuses to go along with this new doctrine of multiculturalism is the worst person of all.

In the West today we've become quite used to seeing confrontations between the alleged lunatic fringe of Islam, and indigenous white men who are trying to defend their culture from foreign influences.

What groups like the EDL do not understand however, is who is really pulling the strings here? Who is behind this? who arranged this fight? because any Roman senator would tell you this is simply the old maxim of divide-and-rule.

The Romans invented this system. They always made sure that every conquered region pushed together tribes who were traditionally hostile to one another. The British copied this method after World War One by redrawing the entire map of the Middle East to make sure that the new boundaries always set one Arab tribe against another: particularly the Kurds.

What we see on the streets of Britain and America today is the same thing: the whole idea is that while you're fighting against Muslims, and they are fighting against you, no-one has the time to stop and think about who actually created this situation, and who their real enemy really is. The rulers of the Middle Ages arranged a never-ending religious war between Catholic and Protestant for precisely the same reason.

Now why must we always think we have an enemy?

Because the ruling group always maintain their position in society by controlling the population through fear.

Think about it. If we don't have an enemy would the public be prepared to pay for the army? Would we be happy to pay for the CIA and MI5 so that they can read our emails? and put a surveillance camera on every street corner?

Big Brother has to have an excuse for watching us all- all the time.

And what they call national security is always the perfect excuse. The moment you make a world at peace it's gone. The Keystone in the arch of ruling class power is gone if we don't have an enemy, so the rich are always going to provide us with an enemy, forever.

And the lesson we need to learn from all of this is that everything in our lives is, and always has been, a rich man's trick.

When people think of ancient Rome they always tend to think about the gladiators in the Roman arena, but something people don't realize is that Roman Amphitheaters were a scam.

They were perhaps the very first big confidence trick in human history played by more cunning rich men upon a naive public.

What Caesar did was to say to the Roman vulgate I will give you gladiatorial games, but only if I can have your votes. And he only offered this bargain because he knew the Vulgate loved the games more than they loved anything.

This is how the Roman Maxim *Panem Et Kirkinses* "Bread and Circuses," became established, because Caesar was the first politician to understand that if you give people what they want they will tolerate being ruled. By this means Julius Caesar made himself into the first dictator whose fortune was protected by a professional army, and everything that every ruler has given us since Caesar has simply been another rich man's trick.

Religion is a rich man's trick. It was invented because wealthy rulers realized the population was getting too big for soldiers to watch over constantly, so they replaced the idea of having many gods with one single God; a simple idea simple men could understand, who could see what everyone was doing all the time.

The idea of one God became the surveillance video of the ancient world. In the Middle Ages the same sort of people grew rich by charging people for the forgiving of sins, and when a new age dawned with the coming of Industrial Revolution they invented new tricks to control the population explosion like … censorship.

Every grown-up knows that there is one law for the rich and one law for the rest, because the justice system is a rich man's trick. Mafia Godfathers like Sam Giancana walked free

from American criminal courts over and over again by taking the Fifth Amendment because it is a criminals' law, and it's the same with everything else.

The media is a rich man's trick. The tax system, because the rich never pay any tax, is a rich man's trick.

Political correctness is a rich man's trick. The murder plot to kill Lady Diana Spencer was a rich man's trick.

And the war on terror; 9/11; the London Tube bombings; the Woolwich terror attack; the Kennedy assassination, all of it is simply another rich man's trick controlling how we think.

Now once again it is very easy at this point to imagine the reaction of conservative politicians who will of course try to laugh this off, and scoff.

Everything is a rich man's trick? Are we seriously suggesting that the COLD WAR was a rich man's trick?

The rich would much rather we didn't think at all, and certainly not about the wise words of the columnist Claire Rayner, who once famously said that the only reason we now have to live under Kings and Queens and Presidents is that in past ages their ancestors were the best thieves.

In the Middle Ages when the King was feeling greedy and wanted to pay for a new mistress or grand new palace he simply sent out his Robber Barons to steal half the herd of every local farmer,

Extract from a TV interview with Professor Antony Sutton

TV Interviewer: Now in your research and analysis and your efforts to bring out the facts about what was going on in our society did you encounter any effort to discourage you to prevent you from bringing out the background of America's involvement in the financing of international communism?

Sutton: Yes very definitely: for example when I was at the Hoover Institution in 1972 I went to Miami Beach to give some testimony before the Republican National Committee, and although a congressman had hand-delivered to the wire services this testimony – which was later printed, the wire services refused to transmit it to the newspapers. Then when I got back to the Hoover Institution in California I was called into the office of the director and I was told in no uncertain terms not to make any more speeches like that, and that this information should not be made public.

TV Interviewer: This was the information that we were giving the Soviet Union the technology to develop its war potential?

Sutton: Oh yes, at that time we were in we were in Vietnam and as you know the Soviets were supplying the North Vietnamese.

TV Interviewer: This was 1972?

Sutton: 1972 yes, and for example, I knew that the Gorky plant, which was built by the Ford Motor Company.. the Gorky plant in Russia produces the GAZ series of vehicles – the GAZ vehicles had been seen on the Ho Chi Min Trail: we were supplying equipment to the Gorky plant in the middle of the Vietnamese war, and these trucks were being used to carry ammunition supplies which were killing American soldiers – now I thought this was morally wrong and I said so in Miami Beach and at the Hoover Institution, and it was this type of information that was suppressed.

and if they complained the Robber Barons would say the King needed to feed the army, or some similar excuse.

That is how it was done then.

But today the ruling class face a different problem.

We now live in an industrial age, and as George Orwell explains in his novel *1984*, if the Machine age was directed solely with the intention of making the common people physically comfortable, in a mega-productive computer controlled epoch we could soon all live like millionaires.

But think what this would mean.

If we're all millionaires we all fly first-class, so the King and the Queen and the President have to wait in a queue with everyone else. And do you honestly believe the Queen of England would wait in a queue? Behind you?

If we're all millionaires we all play golf; the King and the President can't get on the course, and there's no room on their exclusive beach.

Orwell himself would have said the most important single sentence in *1984* was this one.

If it once became general, wealth would confer no distinction.

Our Lords and masters are not going to wait in queues with the rest of us, so the special problem which fat cats face today is how to keep the wheels of Industry turning, because as Orwell explains the Oligarchs have to make use of the masses without significantly raising the general standard of living.

This is a more sophisticated age, so the Robber Barons need a more sophisticated means of stealing most of the wealth, and of keeping most of the common people in poverty.

What the rich face today is a situation in which the common people spend most of their lives on a 9-to-5 treadmill: they make things in factories, they grow things, and harvest them; they teach in the school's; nurse in the hospitals, and as a result of their daily labours a huge mountain of money is produced.

Now the rulers have a problem. How can they keep the ordinary people hard at work so they're too exhausted at the end of every day to think about whether this is a fair system? The solution, as

Sam Giancana explained, is to invent a foreign enemy, a boogeyman, who wants to conquer the whole world.

This becomes a perfect excuse to make people pay for a sophisticated array of increasingly expensive weapons which are made by companies which the fat cats themselves own, and in one neat little scam the modern Robber Baron has a means of stealing most of the wealth produced by Western society, while leaving the common people with just enough crumbs to keep them going.

Every year America's oligarchs take 3 trillion dollars out of the United States economy.

2.3 Trillion with a T: that's 8,000 dollars for every man, woman and child in America.

Extract from a Televised White House briefing given by Donald Rumsfeld during his tenure as Secretary of Defense

RUMSFELD: According to some estimates we cannot track 2.3 trillion dollars in transactions.

This is how the rich have rigged the system so that it benefits them at the expense of everyone else all the time. But in order to keep this fraud going the public must always be convinced of the need for military expenditure – this is where all the phoney terrorism comes in.

And if we want to find out who is behind this ongoing hoax we only have to look at Securacom: the company in charge of World Trade Centre security, who removed all guards and sniffer dogs from the buildings on September 10th so the charges which brought down the towers in controlled explosions could be planted.

If we now ask who is the chief of Securacom?

Who do we find?

Marvin P. Bush, brother of George W. Bush.

Son of the man who orchestrated the plot to assassinate President Kennedy; and grandson of the man who made the family fortune from Auschwitz slave labour.

The Bush family, and their rich friends, have been behind all of it.

During his time as President George W. Bush connived with Tony Blair to introduce a deliberate policy of allowing unbalanced and aggressive Muslims to flood into Western countries.

Marvin P. Bush

They did this in the hope that they would commit atrocities in their adopted countries, and they were actually delighted when the Washington DC sniper and the Fort Hood shootings made headlines because they knew such events would make it easier for the public to swallow the idea that 9/11 was simply more, typical Islamic terrorism.

The truth is that Islam is simply being used like a pawn on a chessboard in a game the fat cats have been playing since World War One.

Seventy years ago they gave us what they called their Hitler project. 50 years ago it was the JFK assassination project. Today we're having to suffer the war on terror project. And when this current lunacy is over they'll have another excuse ready to create yet another phoney war, and yet another Patsy.

If George Orwell was still alive today, and he was asked to comment upon all the significant political events of the last decade it's quite likely he would simply restate the Orwellian definition of totalitarianism: to wit: "a society living by and for continuous warfare in which the ruling caste have ceased to have any real function but succeed in clinging to power through force and fraud" and then ask whether this sounds like the world we live in?

Because it ought to be obvious by now that our seemingly endless economic recessions are being deliberately orchestrated.

In today's world the commodities markets are arranged in such a way that the price of virtually everything, particularly food, hardly ever changes – so how then can it be that the price of oil increased tenfold in the last decade?

Economists are now tacitly agreeing that this was due to 'financialization' which is just a fancy way of saying rich creeps like the Bush family and their merchant banking friends used their Trillionaire fortunes to rig the market.

Why did they do this? Because great entrepreneurs like Stelios Haji-Ioannou, with their budget air travel had managed to break the cartel of the major airlines. Ordinary working families had begun living a Jet-Set lifestyle. The ruling elite of the entire world were simply terrified because a Jet-Set lifestyle is supposed to be the exclusive preserve of the rich.

What would happen to their social status if the whole world were part of the Jet-Set? So the rich arranged for the credit crunch and now working families who used to fly ten times a year can't even afford to use their car.

What George Orwell understood better than anyone is that every age is basically the same: it is always a story in which a small elite group of greedy people cling to unjust power and privileges by practising an ongoing deception upon their followers.

Caesar did it with bread and circuses in the Roman arena. George Bush did it with false flag terrorism on 9/11.

British newspapers have told their readers that the Queen of England is only the 10th richest person in the UK with a fortune of 3 billion, but experts who have calculated her real wealth reckon that her ownership of one sixth of all of the land on planet earth puts her true fortune nearer to 22 trillion.

And they also estimate the true wealth of the Queen's merchant bankers, the Rothschilds, the people who started all of this greed by lending money to the Harrimans and the Morgans, to be at least 100 trillion.

So finally we have to ask what is to be done about all this? for in the case of America it is obvious that in order to honour the memory of President Kennedy Americans are duty-bound to finish his work by finally ending the world wide tyranny of the CIA

The time has come for ordinary Americans to ask their strong men in uniform just exactly what and who they think they are defending?

And they better not take too long about it. Having established Islam in the West in order to provide us with an enemy the elite have recently started on the second phase of their master plan which is to wipe out anyone who is sick or disabled. In Britain this has been manifest in the

ATOS scandal which has stopped all welfare payments to people with terminal illnesses and allowed invalids who in some cases have no limbs to starve to death.

The extermination of anyone considered feeble-minded or infirm was exactly how the Nazi regime began, and now they've started doing it again.

What most amazes me in all of this is the naivety of the good people in the truth movement, who go on and on and on saying they want an independent inquiry.

The Bush family and their rich friends are not going to investigate themselves, and there isn't any authority on earth above that of the ruling class, so it's never going to happen. These people have got the police and the judges and the justice system completely under their control.

The Queen of England cannot be prosecuted for anything, not even genocide, in a Crown Court because the crown courts are hers: she owns British justice.

The only way to change our corrupt system is through revolution. Everyone has to sign up to the revolution now website,* and then the people have to march on Washington just as they did for CIA agent Barack Obama's inauguration: only this time they need to kick him and every other crooked politician out and take power genuinely for the people's sake.

And once again they better not take too long about it, because the last time the rich decided to play a really big trick on the world six million lives were extinguished. Supposing they decide to give us the world's first incidence of phoney nuclear terrorism by dropping an atomic bomb on Cleveland? or Birmingham? or on Chicago? What then?

But perhaps Chicago itself might be a good place to pause and offer a word of warning to the citizens of the United States before they start thinking about the next American Revolution.

We should always remember that Al Capone was seen as a hero by the ordinary working people of his own time because he gave them what they wanted: booze, sex, gambling and drugs. And some Americans have even been candid enough to admit this: "We all cheat…"

It hardly needs saying that Giancana, Marcello and Trafficante would have gone out of business in no time if ordinary Americans hadn't been

Extract from a TV interview with an all-American average punter trying to excuse his booze, sex and gambling addictions

Mr. Average: We all play the numbers; we all go to the Racetrack; you know what I mean? We all cheat a little bit it...

* I was unable to establish the "Revolution Now!" website because the establishment had already taken the domainname to make sure that *nobody* can."

so fond of cocaine, and in the post-war period many writers have noted the way in which the United States not only manifestly tolerated organized crime but even seemed to be enchanted by it.

It's a cultural phenomenon which has led many foreigners to wonder whether there is some sort of latent criminality in the very fabric of American society, because there does seem to be some sort of tacit agreement amongst all Americans that killing a man should always be considered an option if it looks as if he might cost you a large sum of money.

How many times, in how many American movies have we heard this kind of thing?

This film is likely to leave Americans with the impression that JFK was assassinated by a corrupt and brutal ruling class. Perhaps they should ask themselves if they are quite sure that he wasn't simply killed by America?

So it seems that finally we are left with a very simple question.

What kind of society is it which kills its own best men?

Extract from the movie *Network* where the TV Executives begin to plot the assassination of Howard Beale

HACKETT: Suppose we'll have to kill him? I don't suppose you have any ideas on that Diana?
CHRISTENSEN: Well... what would you fellas say to an assassination?
CHARNEY: I hope you don't have any hidden tape machines in this office Frank?!
NELSON: We're talking about a capital crime here.
HACKETT: I'd like to hear some more opinions on that.
CHRISTENSEN: I don't see that we have any option Frank: let's kill the son of a bitch.

AFTERWORD

I think two questions will immediately occur to anyone who has just finished reading this book. The first would be "what terrorism are you referring to?" and the second would be "has the corona virus pandemic been a rich man's trick as well?." Well of course it has been. Everything is a rich man's trick, but let's consider the terrorism first, because where have ISIS gone??

These days people are saying "you hardly hear anything about that anymore." Yes. Exactly. And why not?

The answer is that the influence of my cult YouTube film, upon which this book is based, inspired hordes of quite brilliant people to extraordinary feats of detective work. Having been, as so many have said, "woken up," and made aware that absolutely every single thing we are told by the elite is a confidence trick, they looked at every so-called incidence of terrorism, from 911 to the Boston Bombing, on through Paris, Berlin, Nice and Westminster, and in every single case found video evidence (evidence, that is, which would have won in court) they uploaded to YouTube to prove these were all, without exception, hoaxes, and could only have been the work of the military intelligence agencies who, just as with the Kennedy assassination, were deceiving their own people.

George Orwell would have loved YouTube.

At this moment there is nothing in our world more wonderfully democratic than the public comments section of every YouTube video. In our twenty-first century life it has become a platform from which the common man really can, at last, get a hearing, and Americans in particular have turned to it en masse to share a consistent refrain that my documentary became "a moment of epiphany" in their lives. The tenor of the language used is most interesting; almost like freed slaves. They have written to me saying "I used to be so confused; and naive; and depressed; but since I watched your film/read your book; everything makes sense now" Seen through the prism that absolutely everything is a rich man's trick the way in which, for instance, Cassius Clay was treated over his staunch refusal to go to Vietnam, has now come to make perfect sense to huge numbers of people, and this is making the Establishment

882367 JFK to 911 Everything Is A Rich Man's Trick

increasingly nervous because, as George Carlin famously observed, the last thing they want is a population capable of critical thought.

When Sam Giancana's little brother asked him where it was really at with Vietnam he simply smiled back at him knowingly and remarked "Vietnam is going to make a select few people very, very rich."- Because that was what Vietnam was really all about – juicy military industrial contracts for McDonnell-Douglas and Bell Helicopters; and billions of dollars made from the acquisition of new drug markets. (anyone who is still unsure about this should try asking Ephraim Diveroli and David Packouz)

Sports Writers, in an age where we have witnessed the exploits of Edwin Moses, Aaron Pryor, Noureddine Morceli, Johah Lomu, Shane Warne, Bjorn Borg and John McEnroe generally agree that Cassius Clay was the greatest Athlete that ever lived. Comfortable and often routine-looking victories over such formidable opponents as Doug Jones, Sonny Liston, Cleveland Williams, Oscar Bonavena, Ernie Terrell and Zora Foley made it obvious that even at the level of world class Clay was still in a class of his own: but that didn't mean the all-White Skull & Bones Oligarchs were going to allow "some Nigger" to interfere with their phoney-war Vietnam profits and their plans for world domination.

The disrespect shown to the most outstanding Athlete who ever lived reveals a great deal about the latent contempt all members of a Ruling Class feel for "those below them" no matter how great their achievements, and those who can remember the TV interview with the alleged ordinary soldier who opined that Cassius Clay "ought to be forced to go to Vietnam because he's no better than the rest of us" can now see that that Marine was actually nothing more than a professional Television Actor – just as they can now see the first really critical example of fake news was that "man in the street" who appeared on American TV screens to say he felt Jack Ruby had only done "what any American would have liked to do" by shooting Oswald. (see the Rock 'n' Roll Years 1964 & 1967 on YouTube)

Fake news. Way back In 1964. Who could think it possible? The world was much too innocent to see it then; but for reasons already explained in the text, misleading the public over the Ruby shooting of Oswald was something the rich believed to be an absolutely cardinal aspect of the Kennedy assassination botched cover-up , and it is to be hoped that this new understanding has also enabled Americans to see why Richard Nixon called the students who were murdered on his direct orders during the Kent State killings "campus bums."

Vietnam was conceived to make masses more money for the rich, and Trickie Dickie Nixon was installed in the White House to do just one thing. Keep it going. He was put there to make certain that no Boxing Champions nor horde of Hippies nor anyone else could ever get in the way of the cornucopia

112

called Vietnam – his own reward being that he could sexually abuse as many little girls as he wished (often actually in the White House as Reagan and Bush did later with little boys) in-between fixing up his next hit of Heroin. Perhaps it is as well to remind ourselves here that the four students who were murdered on Nixon's orders: Allison Krause, Jeff Miller, Sandra Scheuer and Will Schroeder, were simply watching a perfectly peaceful protest by unarmed undergraduates during a class break when the National Guard opened fire. As was said at their funeral, it was apparent that they were murdered by their own government simply because they dared to exercise their right to disagree with the leader of their country – something which not even Hitler's Nazis did to their own people.

Even Nixon's own Presidential inquiry into the incident concluded that "the indiscriminate firing, and deaths that followed, were unnecessary, unwarranted and inexcusable." Everybody today really should study the Kent State killings because a thorough understanding of why they happened would help a great many people understand the true reason for the 2020 pandemic.

Those murders by the American government of what were hardly much more than four children showed the world how the richest people think about things. To begin with it's clear they see the crooked politicians they have paid for as being mere instruments of their machinations – they are there to hurt us as much as possible for as long as possible and to take the blame like good little scapegoats whenever things go wrong. They never help the public (when have you ever seen a Politician actually helping anyone?) so why does anyone ever bother with voting? Every time we stagger through yet another four years of "economic recession" and the populace decide "we need a change" the rich simply kick out the Gerald Ford or the Jimmy Carter or the Ronald Reagan or the Donald Trump and replace him with yet another glove puppet. But however replaceable he may be, and it is clear the rich see politicians as being as interchangeable as microwave ovens – his primary duty is to maintain control.

The dirtiest word in the Oligarch ear is mutiny.

Most people live from birth to death without ever knowing how it feels to have power; not even over a school classroom. Hence they can never comprehend the paranoia which goes with leadership. The public are blissfully unaware that the people at the very top live every moment of their lives nervously worrying about when the great unwashed might turn on them; hence the expression "uneasy lies the head that wears the crown." Back in 1963 the American Ruling Class consisted of a small clique of gangsters who owned Oil Fields and Clearing Banks. Try to imagine what was on their minds at that time? They knew their family fortunes had swollen massively due to the use of wartime slave labour which had ended with a six-million deaths Holocaust. They knew they would have to cover this up forever, and because they knew it was all bound to come out under Kennedy they had to kill him – and then cover that up forever. How better to do this than to keep the minds of their brightest and strongest young people firmly fixed on how they were going to avoid the draft?

When they saw the student protests escalating the rich stared out from their stately-home windows at their Lear Jets and private landing-strips and swimming pools and private golf courses and wondered how it would feel to have millions of long-haired students trampling over everything they owned? What does the heavy-handed slaying of the four innocents on the Ohio campus reveal about their rich man's mental state at that time? The greediest, nastiest, dirtiest and most brutal psychopaths were in the midst of setting up an entire world where they could have any girl they wanted whenever they wanted: they weren't about to let Kennedy or any long-haired bunch of dirty peace-loving Hippies spoil it for them because that is how selfish they are.

The super-rich of the 1960's era had become the first Oligarchs in human history to utilize high-speed international private air-travel; which in turn led to the establishing of the intercontinental trade in sex-slaves from every corner of the earth. They would now have to cover this up as well, and for people who were already paranoid this had to mean yet more money would be needed for yet more huge numbers of reliable intelligence agents whose primary function would be to control all media outlets and eliminate anyone who dared to try to find out what was really going on. This was why the true motivation behind the Vietnam conflict was to take control of the South East Asia Golden Triangle drug cartel. It was to provide funds for MI5 and the CIA so that they could efficiently clean up the mess from every child sex orgy and every ritual child sacrifice, and then control the content of every book, pop-record, radio station, television network and feature film.

This, in turn, was what led to the situation wherein writers, film directors and film producers such as myself who wanted to bring out the truth have been unable to get any funding or commissions or distribution deals for their work. It has been said many times that the rich are always willing to do "whatever is necessary" and when it became necessary to corrupt every single channel of mass communication they just went ahead and did it.

But when criminals are making easy money, as I said earlier, they always become lazy and sloppy eventually and start leaving loose ends, and this is what has led to the global pandemic and the true cause of it, the Prince Andrew scandal.

For does anyone really believe it is just a coincidence that the pandemic came hard on the heels of the Prince Andrew Train-Wreck interview? One would think by now that adults would have learned how to add two and two, and to realise that corona-virus is a contingency plan the Globalists had ready all along; just as they "gamed out" the blockade of Cuba many years beforehand. We see a member of the British royal family getting caught with his trousers down, and in a heartbeat the Oligarchs come out with an excuse to freeze the entire world in suspended animation?? Why can't people see this has been done purely because the paranoid upper-crust are now terrified that this 'woke' culture, which now understands the Kent State killings and the shocking treatment meted out to Cassius Clay, and the true nature of phoney terrorism, might just decide it is time for revolution? The public comments on YouTube are filled to bursting with hatred for Prince Andrew, and many siren voices are calling for the gallows to make a return. It is every Oligarch's nightmare. That is why the propaganda about corona virus has reached new levels of absurdity; and also why the police are becoming more confrontational and brutal in every YouTube video.

Everything we have been told about Covid is a filthy lie. The huge numbers of deaths attributed to the virus are a hoax – the authorities have simply been labelling every natural death from old age as a Covid death, and these exaggerations have not been confined only to the elderly.

A young woman I know who works at my local shopping mall told me a friend of hers was kicked in the head by her own horse. She went to her doctor with what she felt might be a mild concussion and he promptly wrote down "Covid19." This will come as no surprise to the truth-seekers of this modern age who are perfectly well aware that all doctors nowadays are basically the whores of big Pharma. Every year they take inducements worth thousands of dollars and euros, usually as holidays to exotic locations, to push the latest wonder-drug on to an unsuspecting public and are hence very easy to bribe – as are the whores in Hollywood who many can see have been paid to claim they have had Covid19. One truly would have to be born yesterday to believe that Donald Trump and Boris Johnson were infected, because it's rather strange that it never killed them is it not??

The pandemic is simply an ongoing falsehood on a scale never known before. The face-masks are pointless and do not work because any physician will tell you that they confer no protection whatsoever after fifteen minutes because the moisture in human breath makes the mask porous. And the virus itself, as huge numbers of critics have pointed out, appears to be hardly much more deadly than common flu. Conservative Member of Parliament Edward Leigh got up on the floor of the House of Commons on January 9th 2021 to ask why he should promote the need for lockdown to his Gainsborough constituents when only four hundred people between the ages of 16 and 60 had died from the virus? (and I do not believe that figure). One wonders just how much more risible all this health advice we are hearing about can become. The media did their level best to try and whip up a sense of outrage that hordes of people were flocking to the beach last summer and boldly ignoring social distancing – especially as the social media gurus were quick to point out that no "spike" in cases happened as a result. Faced with such an unanswerable observation they have changed their tune, and are now claiming that social gatherings at the Coast can be tolerated after all, because the virus doesn't spread at the beach! Covid-19 clearly being an altogether new kind of malady which prefers to get a sun tan.

It is with the same kind of doublethink that they have insisted we must all wear face-masks and stand six-feet apart while professional Footballers hug and kiss each other in a crowded goalmouth. Why do they go on and on with such obviously barefaced contradictions? As I hope it will be clear by now, they are doing this because the rich are afraid. The Aristocracy have not been this nervous since the Roundheads faced-off against the Royalists in 1640.

Try as hard as you possibly can to imagine what the super-rich are saying to each other at this moment? It must feel like only minutes ago that they had complete control over the thinking processes of the entire earth. In the 1980's and 1990's it felt like entire populations were watching soap opera or football. The average working man was able to discuss Dirty Den and little else. Then all of a sudden someone came along and said "Everything is a Rich Man's Trick." And just a heartbeat later Prince Andrew was unmasked as a child molester. Then, as if to confirm that everything is a rich man's trick he told the world he would be willing to assist with the Epstein enquiry, then ran and hid under his mother's skirt and refused to talk to the FBI in a flat-out contradiction of his earlier promise. Try to imagine how many times the Queen's most senior advisors have told her that the Royals seem to be doing all they can to prove me right?

Because the truth is that the Queen of England instigated the pandemic and the mothballing of the entire world (try to imagine how it must feel to have that kind of power) purely in order to save her favourite son from the mob in the street.

She has become so nervous at the way in which the Epstein scandal has refused to go away that her cronies are now dreaming up ever more desperate attempts at sensational headlines which might shift the spotlight off her errant scion, the Oprah Winfrey dialogue with Meghan Markle being the classic example. Absolutely no-one swallowed that story, and even little children were saying they shot themselves in the foot with Piers Morgan's fake resignation melodrama. Lawyers for Epstein's victims were very snappy in pointing out that the only person who would be happy with Oprah's attempts to win an Oscar would be Prince Andrew – and it was most interesting that the UK Broadcaster Lorraine Kelly went out of her way to echo this sentiment. Undoubtedly she feels that Millions of people have become destitute and lost their livelihoods and their businesses and their homes just so that air-miles Andy and his priapic friends can continue enjoying the child sex slaves who frequented Epstein island and gave them oral sex on the Lolita express. Just recently the Internet has been overflowing with videos which show there are now more people living on the streets of Los Angeles than live in proper homes, and in New York shootings and murders have suddenly rocketed back up to 1930's levels. We've had a global pandemic forced upon us which has destroyed millions of lives all because one dirty little royal pervert finally got caught with his pants down.

Never in the field of human conflict have so many suffered so much over something so little.

And why has the Queen done this? Because like every matriarch all she cares about is the continuation of her family line.

The senior politicians and Admirals and Air Marshalls and Scotland Yard Commanders thought they had it knocked. The international Pedophile network they created to entrap and blackmail their political enemies had become a perfect sex-oasis at which old men past their prime could still enjoy the very best sodomy with the youngest little girls. They were demonstrating to the world through the independent inquiry into child sex abuse (IICSA) that they had every top lawyer, judge and politician under their control; for who could ever hurt them, or find out what was really happening, when they had the CIA and MI5 watching their backs every minute? Just at the moment when it really seemed senior figures like Leon Brittan and Lord McAlpine might be unmasked the fake news propaganda machine went in to overdrive, invented the spurious story of the "fantasist" Carl Beech; and no-one has heard the words "UK Parliamentary Paedophile ring" ever since.

The final conclusion of the Independent Inquiry Into Child Sex Abuse was that "no organized international or parliamentary child sex network has ever been shown to exist" and yet Prince Andrew's antics, and everything that has come out from the victims of Jeffrey Epstein and Ghislaine Maxwell, have left no-one in any doubt that an international pedophile network for the servicing of V.I.P clients most assuredly *does* exist; so how come we are not hearing any demands, especially from the UK Labour Party, to re-open the IICSA inquiry??

However, many people have been noticing just recently that the Carl Beech hoax is by no means the only spurious story the media have invented to try and take our minds off child sex abuse and Prince Andrew in particular. Hard on the heels of the Oprah Winfrey interview, which tried, yet again, you notice, to ram the issue of race down our throats for the millionth time, we've had the European Super League story, the Penny Mordaunt/Angela Rayner panto, and the Prince William spat with BBC Broadcaster Martin Bashir, all in the space of a few days. The fake news propaganda machine is currently spinning at peak revs and giving us news management with an intensity never before seen. So why should this be?

Let's begin by demolishing these fake news stories one by one and showing them up for what they really are. The European Super League story was obvious nonsense from the very beginning. When the announcement was first made Jurgen Klopp, Pep Guardiola and all the other Premier League managers said they were given no prior knowledge of the breakaway plan. Now I ask you. Does that make any logical sense? It makes no sense whatsoever. Guardiola and Klopp enjoy as much international respect and prestige as anyone in world sport today. Both are Football legends. How likely does it seem that the owners of their respective clubs would not even bother to inform the manager of the most momentous and earth-changing proposal in the club's entire history? It's hardly very likely now is it? Both of these men were completely humiliated, and had to face the television cameras looking like two errant schoolboys who had forgotten their lesson. The pair of them should have resigned on the spot and it is interesting that they chose not to.

Instantly upon hearing all this I made an unequivocal statement to the effect that it was all just another fake news story, that it would not be carried through and, amidst all the talk of deducted points and huge fines, that it would not effect any Premier League team in any way whatsoever for the remainder of the season. (I might add that when Glasgow Rangers were deemed guilty of bringing the game into disrepute their punishment was to be ejected way down into the Scottish third division – so why was such effective punishment never even mooted against the "big six"?) And what was the upshot? Having clearly been made aware of my prediction the powers-that-be decided within 24 hours to just forget the whole thing. Once they realised the game was up the big six pulled out in unison (Conspiracy?) having clearly never intended any breakaway league in the first place.

So then of course people are left asking "Well, who in this whole world would have the power to manipulate something as titanic in size as the English Premier League purely in order to create yet another distraction story to divert attention away from the Pedophile associates of Prince Andrew?? One would imagine one would have to be the President of the Football Association itself to pull off a hoax of that magnitude."

Indeed. So, who is the current President of the F.A.?

Prince William.

And one needs to realise that this particular farce was just a part of the ongoing hoax the Prince orchestrates on a daily basis with the help of his military intelligence cohorts; who constantly send racist tweets to coloured players (have you noticed that *no-one* is ever prosecuted for these crimes even though they would be simple for the police to track through their online accounts) to try and keep alive the notion that there is a racial issue in sport when there has been no such thing for decades (the monotonous 'Respect' hoardings are utilized for the same ongoing divide-and-rule purpose).

The Penny Mordaunt/Angela Rayner story caught my eye on YouTube because it was entitled "The Public See Through You!" Oooh I thought. What is this? Could there still be just one brave, honest politician in the UK Parliament willing to be the Worm that turns by denouncing the rest for the stooges and whores that they all are? Of course it was nothing of the kind. It purported to be a Parliamentary spat wherein Penny Mordaunt MP was excoriating Angela Rayner MP for daring to suggest that some Conservatives have been on the take during the pandemic. However, if one actually takes the trouble to look into what is being said it swiftly becomes clear that this YouTube video is a staged event, just like the George Floyd killing, serving exactly the same fake news purposes as the ESL story. It is also a rather pathetic attempt by the Tories to introduce Penny Mordaunt, whom they clearly regard as the next Margaret Thatcher (heaven help us) and a possible future PM. Inevitably therefore, the public comments are lachrymal.

Scroll through them, and all you will find is sycophantic tripe like: "ooh isn't Penny Mordaunt an excellent speaker! We should hear more of her!" "Wow! such elegance and poise! This is an exhibition of pure class and eloquence" "A masterclass from Penny: absolutely fab!"

One hardly needs to be a handwriting expert to see that all these comments were written by the same hand; which undoubtedly belonged to some jaundiced, gout-ridden Colonel hiding in the deepest recesses of MI5 headquarters. It is a significant moment in British history because the establishment have now realised that controlling the public comments section of YouTube is crucial to controlling public opinion; and it was with this in mind that I felt I had better add a public comment of my own. What I said went like this:

"I hope the Public *will* be able to see that *both* these women are dirty whores acting out roles assigned to them, because what we actually have here is just another classic example of fake news deftly crafted to try and shift the spotlight off Prince Andrew and his Pedophile woes. The truth, as Penny Mordaunt knows full well, is that *all* politicians in today's world are on the take. They are all essentially MI5 operatives and are being paid huge sums by the Rothschilds and the Royal Family to con the Public remorselessly, day in day out, because if they didn't, in this new information age, the entire population might wake up (as so many have already after watching my movie) to the reality that we are being ruled by a

Fascist Cabal. So please do not be fooled by this oh-so terribly impressive speechifying. It is just a set-up to make Mordaunt look good because the Tories want to sell her as the next PM. In this video she is essentially being an actress; Rayner is in on it; and so is Keir Starmer. They are *all* lying whores and the UK is in big trouble. No-one with a mind of their own would vote for any of the major political parties at this moment in time, because it is obvious they are all being controlled by the money bags."

Now I wonder if anyone can guess the punchline? Having written all this I pressed the 'comment' button. A moment later it appeared in all it's glory right underneath the video. Perfect, I thought. And barely a few seconds later it disappeared. This is the power they have folks. The British Ruling Class simply love to cheat. They do not believe in a level playing field. I therefore sent a copy of my YouTube comment to both Rayner and Mordaunt, challenging both that I was absolutely certain they would not write back. Sure enough, they didn't. And thus is the issue now settled. The UK public, and for that matter every democratic voter on earth, need no longer have any illusions. *Every single politician* in every congress or Parliament building on earth in this age has been effectively corrupted, bribed and controlled by the super-rich. *All* of the political parties are now as bad as each other: and there is absolutely no difference between this age and the tyrannical reign of Charles I.

However Prince William is not confining himself to deceiving his own people merely through using the Football Association as a hall of smoke and mirrors. Only days later we were informed that former Master of the Rolls Lord Dyson had suddenly got it into his head to investigate the infamous 1995 interview of Princess Diana by BBC journalist Martin Bashir because "it was without doubt fraudulently obtained."Whilst everyone was meditating on precisely why a senior Judge should suddenly have such a fit of peek over a story which was 25 years out of date?? Prince William got himself on Television and made some of the most ludicrous claims ever heard in the history of British jurisprudence.

The outline of his case was that 'the lies and fake documents' used to secure the interview, in combination with the "lurid and unsubstantiated" claims the BBC made about the royal family, had "fuelled Princess Diana's paranoia."In making this claim he seems to be inferring that the BBC and Martin Bashir were there, and were responsible for, the period of Diana's post-natal depression, even though this was going on more than a decade before the Television interview ever took place???

Are we to believe Martin Bashir was also responsible for her bulimia?? He gave her the food and then stuck his own fingers down the throat of a Princess to make her vomit it all back up again??

William then goes on to say that the "deceitful way in which the interview was obtained substantially influenced what Diana said" and thus "made his parents relationship even worse" by which he can only mean that Martin Bashir is also to be held responsible for the years and years of Prince Charles barefaced adultery with his mistress Camilla Parker-Bowles. Martin Bashir must possess some truly thaumaturgic powers if he can initiate depression in a woman he has never met, and then inspire her husband, who he had also never met, to become an adulterer.

Not to be left out Prince Harry then weighed in by claiming "our mother lost her life because of this."Oh really? And there was I all this time thinking, like so many other people, that she lost her life because the Queen ordered MI5 assassins to rig her Mercedes Benz so that it crashed in a French Tunnel on the one and only evening in that city when the CCTV system covering the Paris Metro just happened to be out of action. Silly me.

The mainstream media even tried to add some drama to the story by talking about possible forgery and criminal charges the police might want to consider, and they did all this in spite of the fact that someone found a handwritten note Diana herself left behind which said that Bashir "did not show me any documents" and went on "I consented to the Panorama interview without any undue pressure and have *no* regrets concerning the matter" (her emphasis)

Selling out your own mother is about the lowest thing anyone can imagine. And Prince William, just like all those before him who have been raised to believe that all compassion is a form of weakness, manages it with no trouble at all. Talk about live in a Twilight zone of your own making. In attempting to re-write history through this utterly bizarre fake news story the royal family are doing exactly what George Orwell predicted in his dystopian novel *1984* and they themselves are perfectly well aware of this. By this act of selling out his own mother Prince William has made a profound statement: that if the British have to have Totalitarianism, and no freedom whatsoever, in order for the Royal family and the Establishment to survive? well then so be it. Great Britain is now officially Nazi Germany, and we just have to lump it. From beyond the grave, it would appear that the notes Diana left behind i.e. ("they are planning an accident in my car") have shown up the royal family for the liars and Devils they really are. Charles Dickens tried to tell people through his novels that your wicked deeds will always come back to haunt you; and sure enough we now see Princess Diana has her revenge on those who killed her.

This litany of swindles and perversions must have cost half the earth to prepare for public consumption, so it's reasonable to ask once again why the elites have racked up the propaganda efforts during this period? The staff in MI5 must be exhausted. I must confess that I may well be the one to blame.

You see, during the time I was putting this section of the book together I made many notes and also did several interviews myself in which I cast huge doubts on the notion that Ghislaine Maxwell is really in prison awaiting trial. Legions of critics denounced her arrest as a hoax because there was no news footage of her being handcuffed and levered into a police-car (at a place called "Tucked Away," really now?) no mugshot, unlike with Epstein, and those who tried to find her prison number on the website which tells you precisely who is banged up in America drew a blank.

They also cancelled the Live Video Stream to her arraignment, giving the watching world a lot of silly coloured drawings instead: so why would the public have any reason to think her arrest was anything other than just another fake news story, designed to regain control of the narrative? However, I was by no means the only man making this criticism. Look online at any public comments section of a Ghislaine Maxwell video and you will find numerous souls refusing to believe the official narrative on the grounds that we have never seen this woman being arraigned in spite of American Courtrooms being festooned with cameras for the sake of Court TV.

The Establishment therefore tried to allay these criticisms by concocting the latest story that Ghislaine had to go back to be arraigned again to face separate sex-slave trafficking charges; and they used the opportunity to provide some new drawings of what they said was a now slightly underweight Miss Maxwell. But they blew it totally. Because the artist compiling the next round of silly coloured cartoons clearly had not been properly briefed. He produced drawings which allegedly show Ghislaine with hair tumbling over her shoulders and stretching right down her back – in spite of the fact that in the original drawings she is shown as having a virtual skinhead. Nobody, and certainly not a 59-year-old woman, can grow her hair that long that quickly. Hence when they added a photograph with the same length hair I felt it was my duty to point out this rather obvious anomaly; and also drew attention to the fact that the bruised-eye photo looked absolutely nothing like her. And we all now know the outcome.

Just as with the ESL story, only *24 hours* later the announcement came that the trial date was to be moved back yet another five months. This, you see, is why our media has suddenly filled up with an unprecedented level of ridiculous fake news stories. It's a panic attack. They are getting desperate and trying to buy more time because the Ghislaine narrative is false; and somehow, between now and the beginning of the trial, they are going to have to think up some plausible excuse for why she won't be appearing; and this to a cynical public who have never bought the Epstein suicide.

But let us now suppose, purely for argument's sake, that I and the entire legion of critics have somehow got this wrong; that Ghislaine Maxwell really is behind bars in the MDC; and that the trial for child sex-slave trafficking which the whole world is so eagerly anticipating actually goes ahead in November? What then?

The very first question ought to be "isn't justice delayed supposed to be justice denied?" for why should it have taken an entire year for this hearing to come to court? The Prosecution have plenty enough witnesses and evidence of wrong-doing already collated – so why has it been felt necessary to give the Defence such a huge amount of time to prepare? I would argue that the delay-tactics we are seeing with the trial date are exactly the same as the now infamous delaying tactics already demonstrated by Ghislaine Maxwell and also by Jeffrey Epstein during their depositions. The very first order of business must therefore be an undertaking that anyone attempting to *prevaricate* at any stage of the proceedings will face a contempt of court charge which will most definitely carry a long custodial sentence. A ten-year minimum should be imposed, for what is the point in slapping huge fines on people who have all the money in the world at their disposal? However, a thorough understanding of all the implications of the Epstein case does first require a summary of the most crucial details.

To begin with one should remember that the whole thing began when a concerned parent discovered her 14 year-old daughter had gotten hold of three hundred dollars from somewhere: a lot of money to the impecunious families who lived "over the Bridge" in the trailer parks just miles from the opulence of Palm Beach. On learning there were many others she informed the police, whose initial investigation found what was described as "a train" of little girls who were shuttled through Epstein's mansion. When the Palm Beach Police Chief Michael Reiter heard this he took his findings to the State Attorney Barry Krischer, who had a reputation back in 1996 for being a tough prosecutor who liked nothing more than putting bad guys in prison. At first Reiter was emboldened by Krischer's attitude. He exuded confidence, and assured his Police Chief that this was going to be a straightforward conviction due to the overwhelming number of witnesses from "the train" of girls, many of whom by this time were saying half of their school knew what was going on.

The testimony of Courtney Wilde is that Epstein told her he would pay two hundred dollars for every under-age girl she brought to his house. However six months down the line Krischer very abruptly changed his tune. Reiter was informed that the witnesses, who suddenly were not children at all but low-life 'common prostitutes' were no longer credible, and that Epstein was actually a decent fellow who had committed little more than a peccadillo. Reiter was left bewildered as to why the State Attorney's office had become, in a heartbeat, so completely dismissive of a case involving scores of minor children?

Reiter then found being involved in the investigation had introduced a sinister element into his own private life. The way that Defence Attorney Brad Edwards put it was "whenever Epstein was attacked he was known as a character who attacked back" and in his own case Reiter found this meant that as the Chief of Police of Palm Beach County he was himself being put under surveillance. The girls who had informed on Florida's leading Pedophile had reported being followed everywhere by "the same Black Lincoln Navigator," and Reiter now found the very same vehicle tailing his every move, along with the same threatening phone calls the girls were receiving. Now there is no doubt that Jeffrey Epstein was a wealthy man while this was going on. Even so, who in this world has the resources to place an American Chief of Police under surveillance twenty four hours a day?? And who in this entire world would be so fearless as to find the nerve to target a Police Chief for harassment and intimidation??

Reiter then discovered that far from being tried for the sexual molestation of hundreds of under-age victims Epstein was to appear in court charged with just one single count of soliciting prostitution, and the age of the victim was not even mentioned. For this "offence" he was given the most risible sentence in the history of jurisprudence: a year in an an open prison which allowed him to leave the jail for "business hours" (euphemistically called his "work release") so he could carry on trading as normal. In truth it was no punishment whatsoever. He was still molesting girls whilst serving his sentence, and part of the condition of his plea-bargain was a non-prosecution agreement for any and all associates who might have been involved, like his 'girlfriend' Ghislaine Maxwell, whom the victims had described as the 'madam' of the house. Does this begin to sound like 'one law for the rich and one for all the rest'?

But the most pertinent detail was that this was all decided in secret.

Krischer tried to excuse his own behaviour with a public statement in which he said he took the investigation to a grand jury, and that even though witnesses were issued with subpoena it was the jury, and not he, who decided that the indictment would be reduced to just one count of solicitation. He claimed his office had produced a 53-page indictment which was *abandoned after secret negotiations* between Mr. Epstein's lawyers and the office of the U.S. Secretary of Labor, the now notorious Mr. Alex Acosta. Krischer claimed his State Attorney's office was not a party to the meetings, and definitely took no part in the Federal non-prosecution agreement and the *unusual confidentiality arrangement* that kept everything hidden from the victims in violation of the law of the land.

Secret negotiations?? Confidentiality?? Everything hidden?? This is Democracy?

Of course many other literary professionals, most notably the staff of the *Miami Herald*, started asking the same question, and it certainly came as no surprise when Acosta confessed that he had drawn up a lenient plea deal because he was told Epstein "belonged to intelligence" and was "above his pay grade."- Virginia Roberts said during the period she was being flown to London to be the under-age sex-toy of Prince Andrew that Epstein loved to boast about how he "could get away with absolutely anything" because "people owe me favours" and now here was the United States Secretary of Labor, a man, let us not forget, who carries ultimate responsibility for child labor laws and human trafficking, saying he had been ordered to just "leave it alone."And who gave those orders? As a serving U.S. Secretary Acosta had only one immediate boss. His name was Donald Trump. A man who would later tell the world "Epstein's island is a cesspit and you should ask Prince Andrew all about it." How could Donald Trump know this? if he hadn't played in the cesspit himself?

So this is the background to the trial which is supposed to go ahead in November of 2021. Can anyone who has now read this book be so terribly surprised that my biggest fear is that in all this complexity the presiding judge in this case, Alison J. Nathan, might not be able to see the big picture?

Being journalists the staff of the *Miami Herald* have inevitably tended to focus on the harrowing tales of the victims, and so inevitably the public have been left with a sense that the story is about just one dirty old man with money who used his wealth to ensnare lots of little girls for his depraved sexual appetite: oh and he just happened to have a friend called Prince Andrew. The true story, as those who have followed my work are aware, is one of the "hidden hand" pulling the strings from above; just as in World War II.

And the only important question at the trial of Ghislaine Maxwell is whether the owners of those hidden hands will be identified during the proceedings?

Every concerned American at this point should go back and look at the Operation Mockingbird section of *JFK to 911 Everything Is A Rich Man's Trick* because they need to see that the rules under which the Church Committee were operating were a rich man's trick exactly like the farce which allowed Alex Acosta to grant Epstein his sweetheart deal. It's just the richest men making up the rules as they go along like always. During those Senate hearings the spokesman for the CIA was able to ask that the committee go into "executive session" the moment that control of television programmes came up – yet another comfortable euphemism for keeping the most critical details of secret agent infiltration of the mass media a complete mystery to the public.

The American people were never allowed to know, for instance, that the CIA were not only in complete control of every television broadcast, but had for decades been listening in on everybody's private phone calls because they were hand in glove with all the major public communications networks like AT&T.

Back in those days the CIA were in such total control of everything they could listen in on the private conversations of absolutely anyone, and a naive public had no idea. This time around the public are much more aware of this kind of skulduggery, so the question now is whether Judge Nathan is going to allow the intelligence community who controlled Epstein to also control the trial by narrowing the focus? just as they did during the Church committee hearings? Are the world's press going to turn up at the courthouse door to find there is some sinister representative of military intelligence holding the Judge and the Prosecutors on a leash? and leading them away like obedient sheep to some dark closet? out of sight from public scrutiny whenever something which might compromise 'national security' is mentioned?

Is this trial going to be allowed to flounder once again on this catch-all notion that the very same dirty old men who have been molesting and killing these children like mad medieval kings can control, ultimately, every single word which the public are going to hear and read about the proceedings? How can the security of a nation be compromised by the details of how many under age girls a Statesman has raped? Are we meant to believe that they always give the girl the precise launch codes of the Nuclear deterrent while the sodomy is taking place?? And the girl, of course, having a photographic memory, then becomes a military liability??

If this is where we are headed then we may as well forget the whole thing right now, because if the intelligence agencies are allowed to control the trial it is sure to end with just another disgustingly lenient sweetheart deal for Ghislaine Maxwell – for how can there now be any doubt that her own true personal history is that she was simply asked to replace her Father, upon his death, as the chief co-ordinator of the dirty-tricks division of the intelligence cartel which now controls the entire planet.? It is so well-known these days that Robert Maxwell was an intelligence agent for MI5 and Mossad and the KGB and the CIA all at the same time there are even documentary films about it online. Ghislaine simply picked up where her father left off, and used her unique position of power to indulge her own bizarre "Butch Dyke" sex fantasies, which are a well-known theme in modern pornography, wherein an older woman plays a dominant, masculine role with a much younger girl – and her taste in sexual perversions is by no means superfluous in this matter. One can well understand why a highly-sexed woman who has spent her life watching the most powerful men in the world dominate and ravish scores of young helpless girls might become curious about how it must feel to enjoy such unchecked power. And let us not forget that as she grew up with the most powerful people on earth, the British royal family, one of Ghislaine's favourite delights was to demonstrate how to wield power by making Princess Diana cry. It is with these sorts of things in mind that we should be asking whether Judge Nathan will allow the CIA to narrow the focus of the proceedings in exactly the same way as Alex Acosta did when he agreed to have Jeffrey Epstein prosecuted, *not* for the molestation of hundreds of underage girls but only for *one*. This is what the dirty men want. Their entire focus will be on making Ghislaine Maxwell into a scapegoat, exactly as they did with Dr Stephen Ward during the "Profumo Affair," so that she can take the fall and they can get away with it; just like they always do.

Besides being a circuit Judge Alison J. Nathan is also an ordinary citizen of the United States, and she needs to ask herself how it can be, with so much barefaced evidence now on show, that absolutely no-one in either the mainstream media or the Congress of her country has tried to investigate the role played by U.S. and foreign intelligence agencies in the Epstein/Maxwell case? The former Israeli spy Ari Ben-Menashe chose to go on record to reveal that both Epstein and Maxwell were Mossad agents dating all the way back to the 1980's, and many an eyebrow was raised when it transpired that Jeffrey was allowed, only days before beginning his sentence, to fly to Israel "on business." In reflecting on the claims that he so conveniently committed suicide the same cynics have also maintained that had he ever stood in the dock his lawyers would have been legally obliged to delve into the thorny issue as to whether Epstein believed that high-ranking officials sanctioned his crimes because he was providing them with sexual blackmail on specifically targeted dignitaries? which is precisely the same quandary which Ghislaine Maxwell and her lawyers now face; and it is difficult to see how they can wriggle out of this issue when Epstein told so many people that he was indeed a type of "Bounty Hunter" working for the CIA, and that the girls recruited by himself and Ghislaine Maxwell were "forced to have sex with American politicians, business executives and world leaders" Had Epstein made it to court there seems every reason to think that he might have entered a not-guilty plea. There is every reason to think he would have claimed that he was "simply being set-up to be the Patsy for this particular crisis." And what if Ghislaine Maxwell tries the same approach?? Supposing during the trial we hear an exchange which goes something like this?...

JUDGE NATHAN: Miss Maxwell I will not warn you again! If you ask prosecuting counsel even once more to define exactly what a sex toy or a Dildo or a Puppet is or attempt to prevaricate in any way whatsoever I shall hold you in contempt!

GHISLAINE Your honour I am not prevaricating! I simply think that you are not seeing the big picture! and are not aware that history repeats itself! Has no-one ever told you about Phillip Knightley and Stephen Dorrill? Dr Stephen Ward was an MI5 spy during the Profumo affair! He was used by the military intelligence people to get dirt on the Russians! Why would you think it is any different for me? Jeffrey and I were just foot soldiers exactly like Dr Ward. We recruited young girls for blackmail purposes because those were the orders we were given! If you really believe in justice your honour then you must accept that the Queen of England should be standing where I now stand. She is the one most responsible for all of this. Why do you think she has made sure that her own son, Prince Andrew, will not be testifying here? My God, are American memories so short that you've already forgotten Watergate??? The truth about myself and Jeffrey Epstein is that we are exactly the same as Guiseppe Zangara, E. Howard Hunt and Lee Harvey Oswald – we've all been made into Patsies; we're just Pawns on a rich man's chessboard; and If you treat this as just another trial of just another eccentric rich Pedophile it will wind-up becoming *another Nuremberg*! The ones who are truly guilty will not even be identified! let alone punished. Is that what you want? I thought it was part of the American dream that all men are equal before the law?

If this is the kind of thing that comes out at the trial what does Judge Nathan intend to do? Pretend she didn't hear it??

The testimony of Sarah Ransome is cardinal. As a sex-trafficking survivor she has confirmed Virginia Roberts' disclosures that "this was *not* just a sex ring for Jeffrey: this truly was an international sex trafficking ring and *he is just a very small piece in a huge network*" How can any doubts remain as to the true nature and scope of the V.I.P. Pedophile ring since the French arrested Jean-Luc Brunel for flying three 12 year-old Parisiennes to Palm Beach while at the same time Virginia Roberts was being trafficked in the other direction to London? Within days of the Martin Bashir fake news story fizzling away Channel 4 news discovered that Epstein and Maxwell had trafficked girls into the UK over fifty times; and the flight manifests reveal that in most cases they flew the "Lolita Express" into R.A.F. Marham in Norfolk, which is right on the doorstep of the Royal Estate at Sandringham – a revelation which very neatly brings all the heads of the military into the circle of fire: along with an ex-Royal Navy Helicopter Pilot called Prince Andrew.

It seems to me that the record of both the American and British justice systems in this case is so atrocious – they handled Epstein with kid gloves and have not laid a single finger on Prince Andrew: that it really is an insult to the victims to have the case tried in the very same town where much of the abuse took place. One would imagine that child sex abuse by V.I.P.'s on such a grand scale, and over such a lengthy period of time, would have at the very least required the extant authorities to turn a blind eye. And supposing, as seems most likely, there have been high level executives and law-enforcement officials in the New York Metropolitan area involved in the abuse themselves? Such men are hardly likely to want the entire truth to come out, and are strongly motivated to gerrymander the proceedings in some way so as to make sure their own complicity never sees the light of day. Ergo, if the Public really believe that justice for the victims must be paramount in this case? they need to campaign to have the location switched to the European Court of Human Rights in the Hague; and for Ghislaine Maxwell to be prosecuted under the law of *Hostis Humani Generis* (enemy of mankind).

I am not, of course, so naive' as to think that the tentacles of the Fascist Octopus are incapable of reaching into the inner workings of the Hague international court. I am quite sure that the kind of corrupt officials who originally arranged Epstein's sweetheart plea deal can be found, and just as easily bought, in the Netherlands as anywhere else. There are, however, a considerably greater number of sophisticated legal professionals in and around Amsterdam and Paris than there are in New York who have unblemished records dealing in human rights and the prosecution of war criminals like Saif Ghadafi who can intervene in the trial of Ghislaine Maxwell should the whole thing begin to look like a farce, as I expect it to.

So the big question still remains; is Judge Nathan going to be able to see the big picture? and to see that the only way to give Ghislaine Maxwell a fair trial is to understand that every single Congressman, every single Senator, every single European Politician, every Military Leader, every Senior Police Commander and every Prime Minister and President and Business mogul in the entire world should be in the dock with her? Will Nathan be able to see that this case has come about, not because of the perverted sexual tastes of one eccentric Billionaire but because our Western Capitalist system was built *by* Robber Barons *for* Robber Barons??

It is a system, as Claire Rayner observed, designed at the outset by men who in past ages were the cleverest thieves – by men who wanted to make the entire world into a playground wherein every rich thug could kill anyone he wanted, and get away with it; could have sex with anyone he wanted, and get away with it; and steal anything he wanted, and get away with it; and it was because John F. Kennedy wanted to make a better world than this that these kinds of men had him assassinated.

There can be no doubt that both Jeffrey Epstein and Ghislaine Maxwell are two of the most unsavoury characters ever to decorate the world stage; but they are simply being used as pawns in a rich man's game, just like Christine Keeler and Mandy Rice-Davies in the 1960s. Why does anyone think Jeffrey

Epstein, the impoverished son of a Coney-island gardener, was allowed such a meteoric rise through the social strata? The truth is that he was carefully selected, just like Jimmy Savile, because his handlers knew both were priapic-satyrs who couldn't keep their hands off little girls. There were numerous reports about Epstein's 'inappropriate touching' of young girls dating right back to his days at the prestigious Dalton School, hence he, like Savile, was set-up to become the perfect fall-guy. Their rich masters simply gave them all the jet planes and the mansions and the money they needed to establish a global Pedophile network, knowing that if it ever blew up in their faces then it would be Savile and Epstein who would already be neatly in place to take the blame. The corrupt media would simply emblazon their two faces across the television screens and the daily tabloids, while the Bill Clinton's, and Ted Heath's, and Cyril Smith's, and Prince Andrew's, would slither away and hide.

It is simply a rich man's trick no different to a Mafia Don hiring a hitman to kill a business rival. And if he should get caught? then it is always the hitman and not the rich fat cat who takes the rap. As Sam Giancana so helpfully explained such things are a matter of routine with the mob. Why should the setting-up of an international V.I.P. Pedophile network be any less a matter of routine for the British and American governments? and for the secret societies, the Skull & Bones and the Freemasons, who are the real controllers of these institutions.

At this moment all around the world there are millions of little baby girls and boys who are being groomed and prepared to be the next victims of the next LBJ, the next Richard Nixon, the next George Bush, the next Joe McCarthy and the next Prince Andrew. Has the Judge given any thought to them?? Does Alison J. Nathan really believe this sort of thing is all suddenly going to end simply by her handing down to Ghislaine Maxwell a thirty-five year prison sentence? Every single year in this world eight million children go missing. Half a million in the United States alone. Who does Judge Nathan think is kidnapping them?

The American Department of Justice must never forget that every single aspect of their professional life has been laid in place by rich men for rich men. Absolutely everything they are used to dealing with on a daily basis – every habit of thought; every taken-for-granted assumption; every protocol; every tradition and every instinct which makes them feel that this or that is "simply not the done thing" is an idea which wealthy men formulated a long time ago to make certain that they would always get away with it – whatever 'it' may be. It has always been their desire to inculcate in American prosecutors a mentality rather like old-style religious fanatics. It is not so terribly long ago that every courtroom had to believe that God really exists: and that indeed God was the ultimate arbiter in all legal proceedings.

No matter what else might be said in court no defendant could ever sin against the orthodoxy that the Almighty was his judge. Would any twenty first century prosecutor disagree that a contemporary orthodoxy still exists which tends to believe in the idea that there are certain areas one simply may never look into? And that in all matters of culpability it is always the people at the very top, the "Untouchables" who must be given the benefit of the doubt? whether God exists or not? Because what would become of a nations' dignity if it was ever revealed that it has always been run by a bunch of dirty crooks?

It is so easy to imagine the pillars of the American Establishment taking affront at this statement; and insisting that absolutely no concept, and no person, is off-limits or above the law in any American courtroom. Really? Would Judge Alison J. Nathan ever seriously consider the possibility of forcing the Queen of England to testify at Ghislaine Maxwell's trial?? Would the Judge really tell me to my face that this is NOT a no-go area?

After all that we have learned, about the Americans who founded Skull & Bones; about American industrialists building the Nazi war machine; about American industrialists creating Zyklon B gas for the holocaust; about Americans creating phoney wars like Vietnam just to make lucrative profits; and about American Oligarchs arranging the assassination of the best man America ever produced, John Fitzgerald Kennedy, does the American ruling class really deserve the benefit of the doubt?

Francis Richard Conolly June 2021

BIBLIOGRAPHY

George Orwell, *1984*, Penguin Random House, 1948

George Orwel, *Animal Farm*, Penguin Random House, 1945

George Orwell, *The Lion And The Unicorn*, Secker & Warburg, 1941

George Orwell, *Collected Essays*, Secker & Warburg, 1968

Joachim Joesten, *How Kennedy Was Killed:The Full Appalling Story*, Tandem-Dawnay, 1968

Joachim Joesten, Denmark's Day Of Doom, Victor Gollancz, 1939

Joachim Joesten, *Oswald: Assassin Or Fall Guy?*, Carl Marzani, 1967

Joachim Joesten, *Spies And Spy Techniques Since World War Two*, Merlin Press, 1963

Joachim Joesten, *Marina Oswald*, Tandem-Dawnay, 1967

Joachim Joesten, *Oswald: The Truth*, Tandem-Dawnay, 1968

Joachim Joesten, *The Garrison Enquiry: Truth And Consequences*, Tandem-Dawnay, 1967

Joachim Joesten, *The Dark Side Of Lyndon Baines Johnson*, Tandem Dawnay, 1968

Joachim Joesten, *They Call It Intelligence*, Abelard Schuman, 1963

Josiah Thompson, *Six Seconds In Dallas*, Bernard Geis & Assoc., 1967

Penn Jones, *Forgive My Grief*, Penn Jones Books, 1963

David S Lifton, *Best Evidence*, Macmillan, 1980

Mark Lane, *Rush to Judgement*, The Bodley Head, 1966

Mark Lane, *Plausible Denial*, Thunder's Mouth Press, 1991

Sam & Chuck Giancana, *Double Cross*, Macdonald, 1992

Robert J Groden, The Killing Of A President, Bloomsbury, 1993

Victor Marchetti, *The CIA And The Cult Of Intelligence*, Alfred A Knopf, 1974

Barr McClellan, *Blood Money & Power*, Simon & Schuster, 2003

Edward J Epstein, *The Warren Commission And Establishment Of Truth*, Viking Press, 1966

Gerald Posner, *Case Closed*, Random House, 1993

Madelaine D. Brown, *Texas In The Morning*, Conservatory Press, 1997

Bill Sloan & Jean Hill, *The Last Dissenting Witness*, Pelican Books, 1992

David E Scheim, *Contract On America*, Zebra Books, 1983

Anthony Summers, *Not In Your Lifetime*, Little Brown Book Group, 1980

Anthony Summers, *The Secret Life Of J Edgar Hoover*, Pocket Books, 1993

Jim Garrison, *On The Trail Of The Assassins*, Sheridan Square, 1988

Kris Millegan, *Fleshing Out Skull & Bones*, TrineDay, 2003

Webster Tarpley, *George Bush:The Unauthorized Biography*, Progressive Press, 1992

Peter Dale Scott, *Deep Politics and The Death of JFK*, University Of California Press, 1993

Index

A

Accardo, Tony 60
Acheson, David 27
Acheson, Dean 27
Acosta, Alex 124, 125, 127
Adakin, Addy 2
Alderisio, Phil 39, 60, 64, 93
Allen, Richie 11
All The President's Men 9
Alpha 66 55
Anderson, Ian 15
Animal Farm 7
Armgard, Beatrix Wilhelmina (queen) 34
Arnold, Gordon 89, 100
AT&T 32, 46, 125
Avella, Alexander 12
Avery, Dylan 98, 99

B

Baker, Bobby 57
Baldwin, Simeon Eden 27
Banks, Tony 15
Bannatyne, Duncan 15
Barker, Bernard 54, 62, 84
Bashir, Martin 118, 120, 121, 128
Batista, Fulgencio 54
Bedaux, Charles 31
Beech, Carl 117
Beguiled, The 1
Bell, Aubrey 74
Benavidez, Domingo 76
Ben-Menashe, Ari 127
Bhen, Sosthenes 32
Biden, Joe 17

Birch, Dean 60, 84
Birdman of Alcatraz 9
Bismarck, Otto 28
Bissell, Richard 55, 56
Blair, Tony 106
Blood, Money And Power 90
Bogart, Albert 70
Bosch, Orlando 61, 70
Bowers, Lee 20, 71, 93
Brading, Eugene Hale 64
Bragg, Melvyn 15
Branson, Richard 15
Brinkworth, Malcom 10
British Academy of Film and Television Arts 10
British Flim Institute 10
Brittan, Leon 117
Brown, Madelaine Duncan 62, 63
Brown & Root 62
Brunel, Jean-Luc 128
Buchanan, John 9
Bundy, McGeorge 27
Burkley 80
Burkley, George 59, 78
Bush (family) 33, 57, 106, 109
Bush, George H.W. 27, 35, 55, 57, 58, 60, 65, 73, 74, 83, 84, 92-94, 97, 113, 130
Bush, George W. 27, 35, 106, 108
Bush, Prescott Sheldon 28, 31, 32, 35, 46, 47, 94
Butch Cassidy and the Sundance Kid 21
Butler, Smedley Darlington 31, 32, 46

C

Cabell, Charles 56, 60, 62
Cabell, Earle 60, 62
Caesar 103, 108

Cain, Richard 39, 64, 65, 93
Calvey, Claire 2
Camp, Walter 27
Capone, Al 42, 109
Carlin, George 112
Carnegie (family) 21
Carr, Richard Randolph 20, 65
Carter, Amon G. 63
Carter, Cliff 62, 91,
Carter, Jimmy 92, 113
Castro, Fidel 54-57, 66, 99
Central Intelligence Agency (CIA) 10, 12, 42, 45, 47-49, 54-60, 62, 66, 70, 72, 74, 75, 80, 82-84, 86, 88-95, 97-100, 102, 108, 109, 114, 117, 125-127
Cermak, Anton 42, 43
Chaitkin, Anton 9
Charles I 120
Churchill, Winston 37
Clark, Ed 90
Clark, Michelle 84, 85
Clay, Cassius 111, 112, 115
Clemens, Aquila 76
Clinton, Bill 83, 130
Cohn, Harry 40
Collins, Phil 15
Columbo 89
Connally, John 62, 63, 68
Connolly, Billy 16
Conolly, Francis ii, 12, 17, 131
Cool Hand Luke 1
Coolidge, Calvin 41
Cooper, Gary 41
Costello, Frank 42
Costello, John 10
Cox, Jo 11
Crafard, Curtis Laverne (Larry) 70
Craig, Roger 82
Creme, Lol 15

Crenshaw, Charles 74
Crichton, Jack Alston 55, 57, 60, 64, 65
Cronkite, Walter 88

D

Dealey Plaza 20, 73, 84, 91
de Mohrenschildt, George 58, 59, 93
Dickens, Charles 121
Diveroli, Ephraim 112
Dorrill, Stephen 128
Double-Cross 39
Dr. Strangelove 46
Dulles, Allen 24, 29, 55, 56, 57, 61, 66, 92
Dulles brothers 24, 26, 31
Dulles, John Foster 24
Dunkirk (movie) 38
Du Pont (family) 31, 33
Duvalier, Papa Doc 7

E

Edwards, Brad 124
Edward VIII (Hertzog von Windsor) 10, 30
Edward VIII: The Traitor King 10
Epstein, Jeffrey 2, 14, 16, 116, 117, 122-130
Esposito, Joe 40, 41
Estes, Billy Sol 53, 91
Euins, Amos 20, 65
Evarts, William Max 27
Exner, Judith Campbell 51, 52, 66

F

FBI 41, 42, 52, 55, 62, 71, 73, 79, 85, 91, 116
Ferrie, David 62, 64, 65, 83, 92, 96

Floyd, George 119
Ford, Gerald 92
Ford, Henry 33, 46, 104, 113
Freemasons 28, 130

G

Gable, Clark 41
Gabriel, Peter 15
Galloway, Calvin 80
Garrison, Jim 92
Gehlen, Reinhard 45
Genovese, Vito 57, 60, 97
George V 23
Ghadafi, Saif 129
Giancana, Chuck 42, 48, 51, 94
Giancana, Sam 39-42, 46-52, 54,
  56, 59-61, 63, 65, 66, 93-95,
  97, 103, 106, 109, 112, 130
Gill, G. Wray 64
Gingold, Peter 36
Glanges, Evalea 67, 68
Godfather, The 1, 40
Godley, Kevin 15
Goldman, Ron 10
Goldstein, Kurt Julius 36
Goodman, Jason 2
Grant, Cary 41
Greer, William 69
Griggs, George 95
Griggs, Kay Pollard 95-97
Groden, Robert 81
Groven, Enok 15
Guardiola, Pep 118
Gundersen, Ted 97, 98

H

Hackett, Steve 15
Hahn, Emil 25
Haji-Ioannou, Stelios 107

Haldeman, Bob 9
Hankey, John 9
Harrelson, Charles Voyd 59, 65,
  67, 69, 71, 74, 93
Harrelson, Woody 60
Harriman, E.H. 21, 22, 27
Harriman, E. Roland 22
Harriman, W. Averill 22, 26, 27,
  28, 32, 35, 55
Heath, Ted 130
Hemming, Gerry P. 61
Henry VIII 29
Hess, Rudolf 25
Hicks, Jim 70
Hill, Clint 72, 76
Hill, Jean 69
Hindenburg, Paul von 28
Hitler, Adolf 2, 8, 25, 26, 28-38,
  45-47, 54, 57, 63, 86, 92, 96,
  107, 113
Holstrom, Brian 88, 89
Holt, Chauncey 62
Hoover, J. Edgar 41, 42, 53, 55, 57,
  62, 104
Humes, James 79, 80
Humphreys, Murray 40, 41, 52
Hunt, Dorothy Wetzel 84, 85
Hunt, E. Howard 9, 62, 71, 75, 84,
  85, 89, 91, 95, 128
Hunt, Haroldson Lafayette 57, 60,
  63, 64
Hunt, Saint John 89

I

I.G. Farben 33, 36
Isabel, Steve 88, 89

J

Jay, Pierre 27

Jenner, Caitlin 13
Jethro Tull 15
JFK (movie) 88
Johnson, Boris 115
Johnson, Josefa 54
Johnson, Lady Bird 92
Johnson, Lyndon Baines (LBJ) 53,
  54, 57, 62, 63, 65, 76, 90-92,
  130
Jones, Peter 15
Judgement at Nuremberg 25

K

Keeler, Christine 129
Kellerman, Roy 68
Kelly, Lorraine 116
Kennedy assassination 6-11, 20,
  24, 56, 73, 86, 88, 92, 93, 95,
  97, 104, 111, 112
Kennedy, Edward 95
Kennedy, Jacqueline (Jackie) 68,
  76, 78, 81
Kennedy, John Fitzgerald (Jack/
  JFK) ii, 1, 2, 5-11, 19, 20, 24,
  27, 28, 49-53, 55-62, 65-69,
  72-79, 80-86, 88-95, 97, 99,
  100, 104, 106-108, 110-112,
  114, 129, 131
Kennedy, Joseph P. 49, 50, 51, 94,
  95
Kennedy, Robert (Bobby) 6, 49, 50,
  51, 69, 78, 81
Kenny, Edward 80
Keynes, J. Maynard 24
KGB 126
Khrushchev, Nikita 55, 56
Kilduff, Malcolm 74
King, Martin Luther Jr. (MLK) 6
Kinser, John Douglas 54
Klopp, Jurgen 118

Knightley, Phillip 127
Kopechne, Mary Jo 95
Krause, Allison 113
Kriebel, Hermann 25
Krischer, Barry 123, 124

L

Lane, Mark 56, 74, 86
Lansdale, Edward 59, 66, 71
Lanz, Pedro Diaz 61
Lawford, Peter 51
Lawrence, Jack Allen 70, 72
Leigh, Edward 115
Lenin, Vladimir 23
Licavoli, Peter 60
Liddy, G. Gordon 9, 75, 77, 78, 80
Lifton, David 78-80
Liggett, John Melvin 75-78, 80-83
Liggett, Lois 81-83
Loftus, John 9
Loose Change 98
Lord Rothmere 36
Lorenz, Marita 56, 61, 62, 75
Los Angeles Times 47
Lucas, George 15
Luciano, Lucky 44, 45
Lumpkin, George 60, 64

M

Magruder, Jeb 9
Maheu, Robert 56
Maitlis, Emily 14
Mao Tse Tung 48
Marcello, Carlos 60, 63, 64, 109
Marcos, Ferdinand 48
Markle, Meghan 116
Marsloe, Anthony 43, 44
Masferrer, Rolando 64
Maurice, Emil 25

Maxwell, Ghislaine 2, 14, 16, 117, 122-131
Maxwell, Robert 126
McAlpine, Lord 117
McCarthy, Billy 39
McCarthy, Joe 48, 130
McCartney, Paul 16
McClellan, Barr 51, 90, 92
McClendon, Sarah 83
McCloy, John 63
McVeigh, Franklin 27
Meyer, Louis B. 40
MI5 10, 102, 114, 117, 119, 121, 126, 128
MI6 99
Miami Herald 124, 125
Miller, Jeff 113
Monroe, Marilyn 41
Moorman, Mary 20, 88
Mordaunt, Penny 118, 119, 120
Morgan, Piers 116
Morningstar, Robert D. 10, 75
Mossad 126, 127
Moyers, Bill 92
Murchison, Clint 20, 57, 60, 62
Muskie, Edmund 9
Mussolini, Benito 44

N

Nathan, Alison J. 125-131
Network (movie) 110
Nevill, Amanda 10
Nicholson, Harold 25
Nicoletti, Charles 39, 60, 64, 66, 68, 93
1984 7, 101, 105, 121
Nixon, Richard 12, 13, 47, 59, 63, 65, 73, 84, 92, 112, 113, 130
Nix, Orville 5, 72
Norman, Montague Collet 29, 31

Novo-Sampol, Ignacio and Guillermo 61, 65

O

O'Connor, Paul 79, 80
O.J. The Untold Story 10
Omidyar, Pierre 15
One Flew Over The Cuckoo's Nest 1
O'Neill, Francis X. 78, 79
Operation 40 55
Operation Mockingbird 88, 125
Operation Mongoose 55
Operation Northwoods 99
Operation Paperclip 45
Order of Skull & Bones 26, 28, 112, 130, 131
Orwell, George 2, 7, 13, 29, 101, 105, 107, 108, 111, 121
OSS 44
Oswald, Lee Harvey 7, 59, 67, 70, 71, 82, 83, 94, 96, 112, 128
Otero, Rolando 64

P

Packouz, David 112
Parker-Bowles, Camilla 121
Phillips, David Attlee 61, 66, 92
Plumlee, Tosh 62
Poletti, Charles 44
Profumo Affair 127
Pryor, Samuel F. 26, 112

R

Raft, George 41
Ransome, Sarah 128
Rayner, Angela 118-120, 129
Rayner, Claire 104
Reagan, Ronald 113
Reiter, Michael 123, 124

Remington Arms 23, 26
Rense, Jeff 9
Ricca, Paul 40
Rice-Davies, Mandy 129
Rike, Aubrey 79, 90
Rinehart, Gina 15
Roberts, Virginia 125, 128
Robinson, Charlie 2
Rockefeller, John 46
Rockefeller, Percy 27
Rockefeller (family) 21
Rogers, Charles Frederick 65, 71
Rolfe, Hans 37
Romanov, Nicholas 23
Roosevelt, Franklin Delano (FDR) 31, 32, 42, 46
Roselli, John 56, 66, 93
Ross, Robert Gaylon 63
Rothschild (family) 21, 23, 108, 119
Rothstein, Jim 75
Rovics, David 33
Rowland, Arnold 20, 65
Rubinstein, Jacob (Jack Ruby) 47, 59, 63, 70, 82, 83, 94, 96, 112
Ruffalo, Mark 15
Rush to Judgement 86
Russell, William Huntington 26
Russert, Tim 97
Russo, Genco 44
Russo, Joseph 44
Rutherford, Mike 15
Rybka, Henry J. 63

S

Saboteur 38, 39
San Francisco Chronicle 84
Savile, Jimmy 14, 130
Schact, Hjalmar 28, 31, 46
Scheuer, Sandra 113

Schroeder, Will 113
Seavey, Shane 12
Senator, George 96
Sevilla, Joseph 62
Shakespeare, William 7
Shaw, Clay 66
Siebert, William 78
Simkin, John 10
Simpson, Nicole Brown 10
Simpson, Wallis 10, 30
Sinatra, Frank 41, 51, 52
Skoll, Jeff 15
Smith, Cyril 130
Specter, Arlen 80
Spencer, Diana 104, 110, 120, 121, 126
Spielberg, Steven 15
SS Normandie 43
Standard Oil 33, 34, 36
Standley, Jane 101
Starmer, Keir 120
Stellman, Justin 2
Sting 5, 15
Stipe, Michael 15
Stone, Oliver 88, 90
Straw-Cutter, Rick 95, 97
Stroud, Robert F. 9
Sturgis, Frank (Fiorini) 54, 56, 58, 61, 62, 65, 68, 75, 80, 81, 84, 95
Sullivan & Cromwell 24
Sutton, Antony 10, 104

T

Taft, Alphonso 26
Taft, William Howard 27
Tague, James 66, 91
Tarpley, Webster 9
Tater, Robert 70
Tatum, Jack 76

Thatcher, Margaret 119
The Men Who Killed Kennedy 89, 92, 100
Thomas, Albert 76
Thompson, Josiah 8, 35
Thyssen, Fritz 28, 29, 31, 32
Timpone, Patrick 2
Tippit, J.D. 70, 75, 76, 77, 78, 79, 80, 81, 83
Tolson, Clyde 42, 62
Trafficante, Santos 40, 60, 109
Trotsky, Leon 23
Trump, Donald 1, 2, 12, 13, 17, 113, 115, 125

U

Union Bank 31, 32, 47

V

Valle, Eladio del 64, 68, 92
Varandas, Ricky 2
Vizini, Calogero 44
von Lippi, Bernhard 34

W

Wakeman, Rick 15
Walker, George Herbert 28, 31, 32, 35, 55, 65, 73
Wallace, Malcolm 54, 63, 65, 68, 91-93
Walthers, Buddy 70
Ward, Stephen 127, 128
Warren Commission 24, 80
Washington Post 9
Watergate 13, 73, 84, 128
Weatherford, Harry 60, 64, 68
Weber, Friedrich 25
Wenner-Gren, Axel 31
White, Roscoe 70

Whitmeyer, George 60, 64
Wilde, Courtney 123
Windsor, Andrew (prince) 2, 14, 16, 114-119, 125, 128, 130
Windsor, Charles (prince) 121
Windsor, Elizabeth (queen) 1, 10, 105, 108, 109, 116, 128, 131
Windsor, Harry (prince) 30, 121
Windsor, William (prince) 118, 120, 121
Winfrey, Oprah 116, 117
Wobben, Alloys 15
Wojcicki, Susan 1, 12
Woodward, Bob 9

Y

Yarborough, Ralph 62

Z

Zangara, Guiseppe 42, 59, 128
Zapruder, Abraham 66-68, 72, 81, 89, 91
ZR/Rifle 55
Zuckerberg, Mark 15

About the Author

Francis Richard Conolly was born May 23rd 1957 in Wallsend - so named because it denotes the exact spot where the Roman Emperor Hadrian finished his wall. One of his grandparents organized the famous Jarrow March.

His parents were Emmanuel John Conolly, a Shipyard Tradesman, and Anastasia Rose Fortune, a Nurse and Irish immigrant.

Although singled out and praised from the very beginning of his school years as a gifted Artist he hated school so much he regularly played truant, until a brush with the law landed him in Boarding school. Released from what he considered prison aged 16 he studied Art at College and gained entry to St John's University.

Although many claimed he would be "the next Dali" his efforts in the Film department attracted even more attention, with University staff members constantly assailing him to produce Documentaries about them and their departments.

This led to his first professional commission, making a series of Documentaries for the UK health service. But whilst the world seemed ready to accept his talent the BBC, which seemed not to like his Grandfather's anti-Establishment past, did not. Passed over for every Producer's position he tried instead to write screenplays and found himself plagiarized by Paramount Pictures. It was a disaster which did at least force the BBC to sit up and take notice.

Although they could have given him his own sci-fi series (the plagiarized script was for Star Trek) the BBC chose instead to put him into a new Writers competition, which he won. This in turn led to his first Drama Commission, a play about a girl who wakes up to discover she has been buried alive, but somehow still has her mobile phone, and finds that when she calls around her friends to beg them to come and dig her out they are not exactly keen to help a spoiled brat who has been cyber-bullying everyone.

In spite of being hugely well-received, and being aired all over the planet on the BBC world service, it was nonetheless plain that mainstream media were not going to allow FRC to write about the things he wanted to write about. Things came to a head when the BBC tried to force him to take a job writing 'Casualty'. A dreary, predictable, BBC Medi-Drama. He refused and was forced to go supply Teaching to make ends meet.

Although a hugely-admired and respected Physical Education teacher and pro-athlete (he made his debut for York SRC playing against a young Nick Matthew who was soon to become the World Champion) he continued to write screenplays and almost made a breakthrough with Oscar-winning Hollywood Producer David Parfitt, who evinced interest in bringing two of his stories to the big screen.

The project was killed when the world first heard of 911, and Francis soon found his enduring interest in the Kennedy assassination was linking up all too neatly with the government disinformation campaign about what really happened to the Twin Towers. The end result was the cult Youtube movie 'JFK to 911 Everything Is A Rich Man's Trick' which was given the distinction of being the first Documentary ever banned from Youtube in spite of it's achieving way over a Billion hits.